Books by Lois Duncan

Fiction

Five Were Missing
They Never Came Home
A Gift of Magic
I Know What You Did Last Summer
Down a Dark Hall
Summer of Fear
Killing Mr. Griffin
Daughters of Eve
Stranger with My Face

Nonfiction

Peggy
How to Write and Sell Your Personal Experiences
Chapters: My Growth as a Writer

Chapters:

My Growth
as a Writer

Chapters:

My Growth as a Writer

by

Lois Duncan

Little, Brown and Company
BOSTON TORONTO LONDON

Some of the stories and poems included in this volume have been previously published in the following magazines: *Good House-keeping, McCall's, Senior Prom,* and *Seventeen.*

Two stories appeared in the Girl Scouts of the United States of America publication, *American Girl:* "A Gift from Roger," September 1960, and "The Lost Christmas," December 1962. Reprinted by permission of the publisher.

Library of Congress Cataloging in Publication Data

Duncan, Lois, 1934–
    Chapters : my growth as a writer.

    1. Duncan, Lois, 1934–   —Biography.
    2. Novelists, American—20th century—Biography.
    I. Title.
PS3554.U464Z463   813'.54 [B]   81-19339
ISBN 0-316-19552-9   AACR2

10   9   8   7   6   5   4

BP
Book designed by Susan M. Sherman

*Published simultaneously in Canada
by Little, Brown & Company (Canada) Limited*

PRINTED IN THE UNITED STATES OF AMERICA

For my children –

Robin
Kerry
Brett
Don
and Kate

Chapters:

My Growth as a Writer

1

I WAS THIRTEEN YEARS OLD, and it had not been a good day.

To begin with, I had botched up my first-period math test. Then, at noon, I had discovered that my lunch ticket had run out, and I had forgotten to take money to buy another. My combination lock had stuck, so I hadn't been able to get my gym clothes out of my locker and had received another demerit in P.E.

After school I'd gone to the orthodontist to have my braces tightened and been told that I'd have to wear them for at least another year because my teeth weren't lining up properly. Tonight was Carol Johnson's slumber party, and I had not been invited; why, I didn't know—I had always thought Carol liked me.

All in all, I was in a rotten mood as I slammed into the house and dropped my books in a heap on the coffee table.

'Is that you, honey?" Mother called from the kitchen. "There's mail for you on the piano."

I wasn't surprised. I got more mail than most teenagers dreamed of getting, all large manila envelopes addressed in my own handwriting.

But this was something different.

It was a narrow, white envelope with the name and address of a magazine in the top left corner, and when I opened it two pieces of paper fell out. One was a letter, and the other a check for twenty-five dollars.

I stood there, staring at both of them, too stunned to move. Then, slowly, I lifted the letter and read it.

"Mother?" I said weakly. "Mother?" My voice did not carry to the kitchen. I drew in a deep breath and let it out in an explosive shout. "Mother! They want it! They've bought it! *Calling All Girls* has bought my story!"

It was the most incredible moment of my life.

That was many years ago. I am now a grown woman with five children of my own. I'm also a writer of books for young people. Every day I receive letters from people wanting to know how that came to be.

"I want to be a writer," many of them tell me. "How did you become one? Is it hard? Is it fun? Do you earn a lot of money? How do I get started? What courses should I take? What books should I read? Are the stories you write true, or do you make them up? Where do you get your ideas? Where do the characters come from? How do you go about submitting things? How do you get people to publish them?"

For some of these questions, there are concrete answers. If you "want to be a writer" badly enough, you *can* be one. "Is it hard?" Yes. "Is it fun?" Yes. "Do you earn a lot of money?" Not in the beginning years.

"How do I get started?"

A writer "gets started" the day he is born. The mind he brings into the world with him is the amazing machine his stories will come out of, and the more he feeds into it the richer those stories will be.

I cannot remember a time when I did not consider myself a writer. When I was three years old I was dictating stories to my parents, and as soon as I learned to print, I was writing them down myself. I shared a room with my younger brother, and at night I would lie in bed inventing tales to give him nightmares. I would pretend to be the "Moon Fairy," come to deliver the message that the moon was falling toward the earth.

"And what will happen to *me?*" Billy would ask in his quavering little voice.

"You'll be blown up into the sky," the Moon Fairy would tell him. "By the time you come down the world will be gone, so you'll just keep falling forever."

5

"With no breakfast?" poor Billy would scream hysterically.

Eventually, our parents had the good sense to put us in separate rooms.

Aside from tormenting Billy, I had few hobbies. A fat, shy little girl, I was a bookworm and a dreamer. I grew up in Sarasota, Florida, and spent a lot of time playing alone in the woods and on the beaches. I had a secret hideaway in the middle of a bamboo clump. I would bend the bamboo until I could straddle it, and then it would spring up, and I would slide down into the hollow at its heart with green stalks all around me and leaves like lace against my face. I'd hide there and read.

Or I'd ride my bicycle. I would pedal for miles along the beach road with the wind blowing in my face and the sun hot on my hair. There was a special point where I turned the bike off the road and walked it down a little path between the dunes. I parked it there and lay on my back in the sand and listened to the waves crash against the rocks and watched the clouds scud across the sky.

I stored up feelings. I didn't think of it that way then. There was nothing purposeful about those lovely idle hours. But what I found during them, I have still. That is what I mean by feeding material into the story machine. Every experience you have is stored away inside you, to be drawn upon as you need it for your writing. There's an interesting thing about the way the brain functions in regard to memory. The first memories it takes in are the last that it will lose. This is why an elderly person may have trouble recalling a conversation he had two days before, but will remember every detail about a family picnic when he was twelve. The thoughts and feelings you have as a teenager, the information you absorb, the pictures you record upon the screen of your mind, remain with you forever.

So most of my stories are laid in woodland settings. Or in schoolyards. Or by the ocean. And many of my heroines, during their early years, are fat and wear braces and have little brothers whom they tease and treat badly. And there is the magic of the Moon Fairy, translated in more sophisticated novels into witchcraft and astral projection and E.S.P.

My first—and only—poetry recitation was given at age five, and it was a disaster. It was kindergarten show-and-tell time, and since I had forgotten to bring anything to show, I volunteered to recite a "made-up poem."

Amazingly, I can still remember every golden word:

There are stormy winds that blow,
And the ocean's down below,
So let's sing a song of the sea—
For the captain and his boat
With his life and wife afloat,
For they all loved a life that was free.

A torpedo struck the boat.
Life rafts were put afloat,
For the biggest waves were rising very high.
Said the captain to his wife,
"You must jump to save your life,
But here upon the bridge I have to die."

The waves washed the sea-drowned soul
Toward the mast, a pole,
That lay a little southward just ahead.
He washed up upon the shore
And lay there for evermore.
'Twas the noble captain's body. He was dead.

My performance was greeted by a long silence, during which I waited patiently for the deluge of praise I was sure would come.

Instead my teacher said coldly, "You didn't make that up."

I was so surprised that I couldn't think of a thing to answer. I just stood there, staring at her.

"You know lying is wrong," she continued. "It's nice to be able to recite poems, especially such long ones, but it's bad to pretend that you wrote them. Think how the *real* writer would feel if he knew. Someone read that verse to you from a book. Admit it, dear, and you won't be punished."

"I *did* make it up," I whispered. "I like to make up things."

"You did not," the teacher said decidedly. "It's a

well-known poem, and I've heard it many times. Go sit in the corner until you are ready to tell the truth."

I spent the rest of the day in the corner, and it was years before I trusted a teacher again.

But I did continue writing, and when I was ten years old I decided to submit my first typed manuscript to a magazine. The magazine was *Ladies' Home Journal.* I chose it because my mother subscribed to it, and I was able to find the address at the bottom of the "Table of Contents" page.

The story was titled "Fairy in the Woods," and when the editor returned it, it was with a kind letter saying that he appreciated my effort and that the story was a nice one, considering the age of the author, but that his particular publication was not currently in the market for stories about the supernatural. He also informed me that professional writers always enclosed a stamped, self-addressed envelope for their manuscript's possible return.

The warmth of the letter cushioned its impact. I swallowed my disappointment and mailed the story off to another magazine, this time enclosing the return envelope. And I wrote another story and sent it to the *Journal.* By the time that one came back, I had another ready to mail off, and so it continued. I now had a hobby: getting rejection slips. It was painful, but exciting. Each day when other, better-adjusted children were skipping rope and playing hopscotch and going over to play at each other's houses, I was rushing home to check the mail and see which stories had come back from which magazines.

It went on for three full years that way, until that first acceptance letter shattered my perfect record of rejections.

Years later I would write a book called *Hotel for Dogs* that would have the following scene in it:

"Guess what, everybody!" A voice spoke out from the doorway. It was a funny, choked-up sort of voice that seemed to be trying to keep itself steady. "Guess who you're looking at?"

There was a moment of silence. Then Mr. Walker said, "Why, we're looking at a girl named Elizabeth Walker."

He tried to speak lightly, but the words came out sounding strangely uncertain. The girl in the doorway was pale, and her hands were clasped tightly before her. She looked like a person just waking from a dream.

"You're looking," she said, "at Elizabeth Walker, the published writer!"

That scene leapt, fullblown, from my own bank of memories.

How do you become a writer? The road is a long one. If you're lucky you'll keep progressing along it for a lifetime. Since each of us is different, it's impossible to lay out a road map that will work for everyone. The best I can do is to show you how it was for me as I moved step by step through my teen years, dreaming my dreams and writing my stories. They are far from masterpieces. They are the fumbling efforts of a beginning writer to become a better writer, but I learned from each of them.

Perhaps you can too.

The Fairy in the Woods
written at age 10

Sandy stood quietly watching her, watching with large, blue eyes because he was afraid she might disappear like one of those fairy lights that you sometimes see on summer nights. He did not want her to disappear, she was so beautiful. Her hair was brown, a soft brown, like the brown of a pine tree when the sap begins to run, and her eyes were dark and full of secrets like the woods.

"Excuse me," said Sandy softly, "but are you a fairy?"

He spoke softly because he did not want to startle her, but she was not the least bit startled, and she smiled at him as if she had known all along that he was there. She held out her hand to him, and Sandy did not need to ask again if she were a fairy.

"The woods are misty," he said.

"It's because of the dream dust, you know."

"Yes, I know," and he realized suddenly that he really had known but had only forgotten. You remember all sorts of things when you are with a fairy.

"I am five years old," said Sandy. "Tomorrow I will be six."

"That's why I came."

"Because I am six tomorrow?"

"No, because you are five today."

"I bet I know how old you are!" he shouted. "You are a million billion years old!"

"You are right. And yet, I was born only yesterday."

And she laughed, a clear musical laugh, and Sandy laughed too, scarcely knowing what he was laughing at. They ran hand in hand through the woods, laughing as they ran, and the birds called them, not chirping and trilling but calling and asking them what they were laughing at. But Sandy did not know, and the fairy did not care, so they ran on, and the birds laughed too until the woods rang with their laughter.

"What is that around your neck?" asked Sandy.

"A necklace made of dewdrops."

"It's very beautiful."

"It should be. It was polished with moonbeams."

"I want it!"

"So do I!" And they laughed again.

A rabbit hopped out of the bushes.

"Stop!" he cried. "Stop and talk to me!"

"No!" cried the fairy.

"No!" cried Sandy as they ran on.

"But life is so long!" called the rabbit. "Surely, you have a minute?"

"Life is short!" cried the fairy.

"Too short!" echoed Sandy as if he had discovered it for the first time.

The warm afternoon sunshine was beginning to dim as they stopped by the edge of the woods.

"Again tomorrow?" asked Sandy.

"No, never again."

"I shall come and hunt for you!"

"But you will not find me."

"Why?"

"Because you will be six years old."

"But I love you! I love you!" cried Sandy, close to tears. "I *will* find you! I *must* find you!"

But the fairy was gone, and the sun was low in the west.

"It was a dream, Sandy," said his mother firmly the next morning. "She couldn't have been real."

Sandy's eyes were confused, troubled and a little frightened.

"No," he said slowly, "she couldn't have been real."

And at once he felt older and wiser, but a little sad, as if he was losing something very dear, something that he wanted to keep. His throat hurt as if he were going to cry, but he knew that he wouldn't. It was just a dull, throbbing ache that seemed to come from way down inside of him.

The sunbeams were dancing merrily on the windowsill, and birds chirped and trilled from somewhere in the apple tree on the lawn. The presents lay wrapped and waiting on the dining room table, and suddenly the fairy lady, along with the new-found pain, was lost—lost forever—in the glorious new feeling of being grown up.

ALTHOUGH I SUBMITTED IT many places, "The Fairy in the Woods" was never published. I couldn't understand it, because I thought it was good. I read it today as an adult, and I still think it's good—for a ten-year-old. But it is not the polished work of a professional.

If I had sent the story to a children's magazine it might have been accepted. I didn't think of that. I submitted it, instead, to the top magazines in the country, one after another, and, of course, it was rejected. It could not compete in those markets, and adults are not particularly interested in fairy tales.

So, was it wasted, that story? No, it wasn't, for I learned through writing it. For one thing, I experienced that day what it felt like to play God. I created a world—a woodland world, peopled with birds and rabbits, and dusted with magic—and into that world I placed a boy named Sandy. I spent a lot of time choosing a name for him, because I wanted him to fit into the woods as if he belonged there. A solid, formal name would not have been right for him. He could not have been Alfred or Jerome or George. He *had* to be Sandy, so that he could slip right in with the other natural elements like the pine trees and thickets and mist. And should I name the fairy also? I worried over that point and decided at last that she should be nameless. If I gave her a name, I would be making her real, and I wanted the reader to be uncertain about that. Was she, perhaps, as Sandy's mother suggested, just a dream?

No, that story was not wasted, and neither were the poems and stories I wrote in the three years following. Nobody published them, but creating them made me happy. I still have notebooks I filled during that time, and as I leaf through them, I am ten and eleven and twelve again, torn like Sandy between the desire to grow up quickly and become an adult, and a reluctance to leave the fairy-tale world of childhood.

Here are some poems from those years:

Evening
written at age 10

Evening tiptoed into the wood
Wearing his sandals and velvet hood,
> *Wrapping around him his cape.*
And then he drew forth his bag of night
And loosened the string he had tied so tight,
> *Letting the stars escape.*

At last, in a shower of silver gleams,
He emptied his pockets, all full of dreams,
    And he shone the moon up bright.
Then as the nightbirds began to call,
He drew them together and wrapped them all
    In his blanket of velvet night.

Beliefs
written at age 11

I used to think the stars were diamonds
Of a rich and crafty merchant
And when once he became angry
He had tossed them to the blue.
And that the silver moonbeams
Were the fairies' shining stairways
That they joyfully descended
When they scattered morning dew.

I thought the large and fluffy clouds
Were fairies' herds of cattle
And the scattered little white ones
Were a fairy's herd of sheep,
And the impish, naughty pink ones
Were the elves disguised to fool me,
And they held the Sandman's sandbags
While he put me fast to sleep.

And I used to think each raindrop
Was a sorry angel's teardrop,
And he now was crying bitterly
Because he couldn't fly.

He had torn his wings to tatters
In the brier patch on the meadow
When he stopped to free a captive wren.
(He could not pass her by.)

But now I know my diamonds
Are only far off planets.
The moonbeams are reflections,
And the clouds collect the rain.
But I've also learned that fairies
Are the fancies of your childhood,
So I wish—I wish my fairies—
Would come back to me again.

The Water Nymph
written at age 12

He might have been an angel, and he might have been a
*   devil,*
And he might have been a fairyman, it's very hard to say.
But he was dancing through the evening in the rushes by
*   the river*
With the evening breezes blowing at the closing of the day.

If he was a kind of angel he most surely was a bad one
For he danced out through the rushes where the evening
*   dew was cold.*
And if he was a devil, then the sun is fond of devils,
For its last small ray came streaming down to bathe his head
*   in gold.*

So he must have been a fairy. But it's strange about the
*   fairies,*
For a fairyman is ended with the coming of the dawn.
There was something in his dancing that I knew would last
*   forever,*
Always dancing on forever, even after he vas gone.

The hills were bathed in shadows, but I still could see him
*   dancing,*
Just a stirring of the rushes and a breathing on the hill.
Then the quiet dark descended, like a blanket dropped from
*   heaven.*
The night had claimed its glory, and the dancing form was
*   still.*

Are those "good poetry"? Not by literary stan-
dards. If I'd shown them to my teacher, I'm sure she
would have pointed out all kinds of things wrong
with them. Actually, they don't make much sense. If
"Evening" is carrying a "bag of night," how could it
also be a "blanket"? And how can his "hood" and
"night" be made out of the same material? Shouldn't
the hood be made out of something else? Silk,
perhaps? But *silk* has only one beat, and that spot in
the poem needs two. Maybe *silken* would work there.
But, then, silk isn't the sort of stuff you make hoods
out of either, is it? And see how many times I used
the word *night* in the same short poem? I even have
"nightbirds" calling at "night." When else would the
things call? If it were morning, they would be
"morning birds."

In "Beliefs" the rhythm is off. And in "The Water Nymph" I keep overusing certain words like *evening* and *rushes*. Couldn't I have found an occasional substitute so they wouldn't keep repeating themselves in the reader's head like gongs?

Thank heaven, I didn't show the poems to my English teacher. I wasn't then at a point where I could have made use of constructive criticism. Poetry was flowing out of me in a natural way with as little effort as breathing, and I was playing with words as though they were toys. I could see in my own mind's eye the fairies tripping merrily down their moonbeams, and Evening huddled in his cloak, and the nymph's slender figure leaping and twirling at the river's edge in the final shaft of afternoon sunlight. I thought they were beautiful. I didn't want or need right then to have someone ruin them for me by telling me to count my word beats or eliminate a few *nights*.

And without instruction, just in the process of writing, I was learning. That is evident when you compare the poem written at ten with the one written at twelve. Something positive was occurring. I was becoming more comfortable with the images I was creating. The word-pictures were more vivid, and I was beginning to develop a surer sense of rhythm and to experiment with longer, more intricate lines. It was child's poetry still, but better child's poetry than it had been.

* * *

Then my dog was run over, and I discovered death.

My dog's name was Ginger. She was an Irish terrier, and I had gotten her on my seventh birthday. I was almost thirteen the spring she was killed. My parents, who were magazine photographers, were out of town on assignment, and Billy and I were being babysat by our grandmother. When I got up that morning I called Ginger so I could feed her, but she didn't come. When I went out to catch the school bus, she was lying in the road with her head crushed.

The agony of that day was intensified by the fact that my mother wasn't there to comfort me. My grandmother tried, but it was not the same. I remember overhearing her on the phone with a friend, calling off their afternoon bridge game.

"Lois is so upset," she told her apologetically. "You know how devastating life's little tragedies can be at her age."

I was furious. A *little* tragedy! Was *that* what it seemed to her?

"If this is a 'little' tragedy," I remember crying, "how do people ever live through big ones?"

"With difficulty," she said quietly.

In retrospect, I can see how that question must have affected her, as she had lost her younger daughter during the past year and her husband several years before. At the time, however, all I could think about was how heartless she was. Ginger was dead, and my grandmother considered it unimportant.

When my parents returned two days later, Mother wept with me.

"Why?" I kept asking. "Why did it have to happen? She was such a good dog!"

"There must be a reason," Mother told me. "You can't see it now, and I can't either, but it must be there. Maybe someday, when you look back, you will find that something good did come of this."

"That's impossible!" I cried.

But I grew up a bit that day. It was quite a while before I again felt like writing, but when I did, my previous subject matter seemed shallow and unimportant. I wrote a story called "The Reason." And a year later, when I submitted it to a youth publication, they bought it.

The Reason
written at age 13,
published in Senior Prom, *December 1949*

Up until a few moments ago his mother had been there, but now she had slipped from the room, very quietly, thinking he was asleep. The boy was glad she was gone. A woman was warm and comforting but he did not want to be comforted. A woman's hands were gentle and her crooning could partially smooth away the pain, but he was no longer a child and he wanted to bear his pain. He was suddenly a man, and he had no need for women.

The boy lay stiffly on the bed and felt the cold cut easily through the coarse blanket and wrap itself about his body. He thought about the calf and shut his eyes and imagined himself in the barn, sprawled beside it in the warm, sweet-smelling hay. He could almost feel the heaving of its hot, awkward body and smell the strangely beautiful smell that he always connected with it. Of course, all calves smelled a little the same, and they were all built in much the same way, but somehow this one had always been different. This one was his.

It was the first time he had ever been allowed to witness a birth. Always before he had been too little, but because it was to be his calf and because he was now quite old, all of twelve, his father had said it was all right. Of course, his mother had minded. She hadn't wanted him to see. She herself had gone inside the inn and stayed while the actual miracle was taking place.

The old cow had lain on her side in the hay, gasping a little—and then it had happened. There had been one crucial, heart-stopping moment, a moment in which the stable had seemed to vibrate with pain. And then, little and wet and helpless, there had been the calf. The boy had crept close and stretched out his hand and touched it, very gently, and it had been real and alive under his touch. It was then he had known that it was his calf, really his.

Now he turned and pressed his face deeper into the pillow. He was a man. He had loved something and it was gone. Such things happened all the time to men. They did not cry. They did not act like children.

At first he had been able to carry the calf, but to his disgust it had grown faster than he. Somehow they had been alike. They had both had knobby knees and both had liked to drink from streams and run in clover. And they had both been born.

Lying there, he tried to imagine himself being born. He tried to imagine his quiet, comforting mother experiencing that brief moment of exulting pain that he had witnessed, but he couldn't. Still, it must have happened.

And someday he must die—as the calf had died.

"Why?" he thought. "Why? Why?"

Even his father had not known why. There had seemed no reason for it. None of the other cattle had been sick, only his calf. For two nights and three days they had worked with it, struggling against the icy wind to the stable where it had lain, feeding it by hand, sitting with it by night. And today it had died, quietly.

They had carried it out to the edge of the woods, his father and he, and left it. The wind had been stinging upon their backs as they stumbled along with it. The boy had wanted to dig a grave, but the ground had been too hard, and he had wanted to stay for a while beside it, there in the protective shelter of the trees, but his father had not let him. Instead they had returned to the inn. They had fed the other animals. They had eaten dinner and washed the dishes and seen to the guests. There had been no reason why the calf should have died. No reason at all.

The boy was glad that his mother was gone. She was like all women. She stroked his forehead and dried his tears and told him there had to be a reason, that there was a reason for everything, that maybe when he was grown and thought back on it, he would see a reason and be able to understand.

It was his mother who had given it away about the empty stall in the stable when the people had come to the door. His father would never have thought of it. In fact, he had already told them there was no room, that the inn was filled. The people had turned to leave when his mother came forward and touched his father's arm.

"Wait," she had said urgently. "You can't! You can't send them out on a night like this. Especially a woman who is—is—"

His father had shaken his head, regretfully but firmly.

"There is no room," he had said.

The night was very cold. The wind, blowing in through the open door of the inn, was a sharp, icy wind.

"What about the stable?" his mother had suggested quietly. "The calf died today. There is an empty stall. It would be better than bearing a child outside without shelter, out in the night, in the cold."

There was a moment of silence and the boy had tried to speak, but the words would not leave his throat. He wanted to do something to stop it. He wanted to scream bitterly, "The calf is dead! Isn't it lucky the calf is dead! What would we do if the calf were not dead!" He wanted to laugh wildly and convulsively, but he could not.

His mother's face was gentle, and the woman turned to her with quiet, trusting eyes. A look passed between them.

His mother had said, "You are very blessed."

The woman had said, "I know."

The boy had broken away and fled to his room. He lay very still upon his bed, trying to weep, but the tears would not come. There was only pain.

The boy felt his thin body stiffen with fury against his mother. She had acted almost as though it were a lucky thing that the calf had died! His calf!

The night was still. The only sound was that of the wind singing around the corners of the inn. After a while the wind seemed to die down and even this sound stopped. Everything was silent, a breathless sort of silence. All the world seemed waiting for something.

The boy felt the waiting, the tension. He felt it in the air and in the pressure of the blanket upon his body and in the pulsing of his blood as it pounded through his veins. He heard it in the night and in the cold and in the stillness. In the terrible stillness he could hear the night singing—a strange, bewildering song which echoed louder and louder in his ears. He heard his breath, and his breath was singing, and he felt a pressure like the weight of the world.

Suddenly his hate and pain vanished in a tremendous realization! The moment was an exact duplicate, only a thousand times over, of that moment out in the hay when the cow had given birth. It was a moment of terrible glorious exulting pain, something he could not understand and did not wish to understand but could only feel.

The door opened and his mother came in. She crossed over to his bed and spoke to him softly.

"Are you awake?" she whispered.

He heard her perfectly, but he did not answer for fear he might break the glorious spell that hung upon him.

She turned and went to the window and stood there a long time, looking out. Finally she came back and put her hand on his arm.

"Are you awake?" she asked again.

The boy sat up and put his feet upon the floor. The boards were cold beneath his feet, but he hardly felt them.

His mother said, "Hurry to the window. Over our stable is the most wondrous star ever to be seen in Bethlehem!"

He crossed to the window. The singing was all about him and within him, throbbing in his ears, and the sky above the stable was burning as bright as day.

"It's almost," he whispered to his mother, "as if the whole world were beginning!"

And then, quite suddenly, he knew the reason.

3

IT'S INTERESTING TO NOTE that in every story I wrote during those early years, the main character was a boy. I had always wanted to be a boy. Boys didn't have to be pretty. An overweight boy was "husky," while an overweight girl was "fat." I dressed like a boy as often as my mother would let me and almost pulled my arm out of the socket trying to kiss my elbow, which I'd heard was the magic formula for changing sex. Needless to say, I was unsuccessful.

What I couldn't accomplish in real life, I *could* do on paper. All of my stories were written from a boy's viewpoint.

Then when I was thirteen a miracle occurred: I lost my baby fat. I don't know how it happened; it just fell away. I looked in the mirror, and suddenly there were bones and hollows in all the places where there used to be bulges. The following year the braces which I'd worn since the age of seven came off at last, and I graduated to a nighttime retainer. Soon after that a boy named Roger invited me to go to the movies, and I decided that being a girl wasn't such a bad thing.

It was a long time before I wrote from a boy's viewpoint again.

As I matured, so did my writing. As with any other activity, if you keep hacking away at it day after day, you're bound to make some progress. When you compare "The Fairy in the Woods" with "The Reason," it's obvious that the later is the better story. But, why?

For one thing, I tackled stronger subject matter. There's also the fact that the construction is more sophisticated. "The Fairy in the Woods" is written very simply. We follow Sandy through his afternoon romp and wind up with his talk with his mother. The only things we know about him are those that occur during that particular time period. In "The Reason," however, although the only thing our main character actually does is get out of bed and look out the window, we learn all the events that led up to this. We do this through a flashback. I had the boy reach back with his mind and recall the birth of the calf, the fun he had playing with it, its sickness and death, and the arrival of the couple at the inn. Without this background material, the sight of the star over the stable wouldn't have meant much as the story's climax.

"The Reason" has its weaknesses. I used far too many adjectives, and repeated the same words over and over. In the second paragraph, for instance, I used *smell* four times. I got pretty flowery, and I threw in some ridiculous observations because I thought they were poetic. "He was suddenly a man, and he had no need for women." How much sense does that make? What I meant, of course, was that he had no need of being *mothered* by a woman. If I were writing that story today, I would do a lot of editing.

When you're a writer, there is always the question of how much to tell your reader and how much to let him figure out for himself. You don't want to insult him by overexplaining. At the same time, you don't want to leave him staring blankly at the last page, wondering what the point was. With "The Reason," I had a choice to make. Should I have the couple identify themselves: "Hello, I'm Joseph, and this is my pregnant wife, Mary. We need a room"? I decided I wouldn't because I would be giving away too much too soon. But what if the reader wasn't bright enough to catch on? Maybe he thought that the big light in the sky was a spaceship? I tried to protect myself from that possibility by having the mother use the name of the place: Bethlehem.

Once my story was accepted, I had another decision to make. My name was Lois Duncan Steinmetz, and I had been named after my mother. When my story appeared in print, I didn't want everybody to think that Mother had written it!

We discussed the situation, and Mother wasn't too keen on the idea of changing her own name so it wouldn't be confused with mine. She suggested that I drop *Steinmetz* and use my first and middle names to write under. The idea pleased me. Duncan had been my grandmother's maiden name, and it conjured up romantic visions of brightly kilted Scotsmen marching over rolling hills to the blare of bagpipes. So I wrote the editor of *Senior Prom* and told her that I was going to publish under a pseudonym, *Lois Duncan*.

Those first magazine sales went to my head. The local newspaper ran an article about me, and I went floating around, feeling famous, wishing somebody would ask for my autograph. When nobody did, I went back to the typewriter and wrote another story. I made this one very dramatic. It was about a cheating woman, murdered by her jealous husband. I submitted it to *Senior Prom* and sat back to wait for my check.

It didn't come.

Instead, the story came back by return mail with a letter saying, "We can't use this. It's stilted and unnatural. You're trying too hard."

Trying too hard! How could anyone try too hard to be successful?

I wrote another story, and this one came back also.

There wasn't even a letter, just a printed rejection slip.

What had happened? I asked myself frantically. It had all been so wonderful! Could it really be over? Was it possible that I would never have another story published as long as I lived?

After three more rejections, it certainly started to look that way.

Meanwhile, I was spending so much time and energy at the typewriter that I was falling down in all my classes. My English teacher loved me, but nobody else did. I was dipping toward a D in geometry, and—dear Lord, was it really possible? —I was *flunking* home economics. I, Miss Superbrain, the published author, was getting an F!

And now, I guess, is the time to explain that I have never been Miss Superbrain. I'm lopsided. I have always been good with words, but I make up for that by my lack of ability in many other areas. I am poor at math and science. I have a total block against foreign languages. And I am terrible at sports. If somebody tosses a ball to me, my automatic response is to cover my face and duck.

There is something else wrong as well, something that as a teenager I was so embarrassed about that I couldn't even discuss it with my parents. I have almost no visual memory. I cannot remember what things and people look like. If I meet someone new and analyze his looks, telling myself, "He has red hair and freckles and a hook nose," I will remember the description, but I won't be able to bring to mind a picture of the face.

If two people fit the same description, I'm lost. I can't tell them apart.

This may sound like a minor problem, even an amusing one, but it can make life a nightmare. My first year in junior high school, I built a reputation as a snob because I never spoke to people in the halls or lunchroom. I wasn't sure enough of their identities to risk it. What if I thought I knew them and really didn't? What if I called them by the wrong names?

I had the same problem with teachers. I can recall one traumatic occasion when Mr. Strode, the principal, stuck his head out into the hall as I was passing and said, "Lois, if you're headed for the lunchroom, would you please ask Mrs. Romero to stop by my office for a moment?"

Mrs. Romero was my math teacher. She had brown hair and glasses. Miss Jacobs, my science teacher, also had brown hair and glasses. When I reached the cafeteria, two women with glasses and brown hair were sitting together at one of the tables. Despite the fact that I had taken classes from them for a whole semester, I couldn't tell them apart.

I went to the table and stood there, hoping desperately that one of them would say something to give me a clue, something like, "Are you ready for the science test tomorrow?" No such luck. They simply smiled pleasantly and said, "Hello," and sat there, waiting for me to tell them what I wanted.

The silence deepened. I was ready to turn and leave with the message undelivered when one woman raised her hand to adjust her glasses. It was her left hand, and there was a ring on the fourth finger!

Relief flooded through me.

"Mr. Strode wants to see you, *Mrs.* Romero!" I announced triumphantly.

My secret was safe. I had not made a fool of myself.

Add to these defects my shyness and the fact that I spent so many years being fat and bucktoothed, and you can see why it was so terribly important to me to be a success at something. I had had one taste of glory, and I wanted another. In fact, I had pretty much decided that writing was going to be my career.

The fourth rejection from *Senior Prom* came in the form of the usual little printed slip saying, "Sorry, we can't use this," but at the bottom the editor had written a personal note.

"This story and the last few you sent us are too contrived," it said. "You've lost the naturalness of your earlier submissions. Reach into your own life. Write about something you yourself have experienced."

Contrived? Those spontaneous outpourings about love, lust and murder? I was so upset by the criticism that I threw a towel over the typewriter and vowed never to write again. By the following day, however, I had reread the rejected manuscript and come to realize that the editor was right. I was writing on subjects about which I knew nothing. I had never murdered anybody, nor had I had a love-affair. The most dramatic thing that had happened to me lately was flunking Home Ec.

The next thing I submitted was a short personal-experience piece called "Home Economics Report," and not only did *Senior Prom* buy it, they raised the purchase price to $50.

Home Economics Report
written at age 14,
published in Senior Prom, *1950*

Name: Lois Duncan

Age: 14

Course: Sewing

Project: Making a skirt

Previous experience: None

1st Day: Started project with great vigor. Spent ten minutes trying to thread needle, because was unable to decide which end of needle thread was supposed to enter. Bit off thread three times. Chipped front tooth. Swallowed last piece of bitten thread and left class for drink of water. Returned, greatly refreshed, and found that I had been threading straight pin.

2nd Day: Successfully threaded needle.

3rd Day: Removed pattern from envelope. Found pattern had little holes in it. Mended holes with Scotch tape.

4th Day: Pinned pattern to cloth. Cloth is a plaid. After cutting, found that plaid on front of skirt goes up and down, and plaid on back of skirt goes sideways.

5th Day: Basted skirt today. Sewed all period before discovering that I had forgotten to knot thread.

6th Day: Played it safe. Knotted thread at *both* ends to be sure it held. Chipped other front tooth.

7th Day: Cut out pocket. Was so careful to match plaids that I had to cut it from the center of a 5' piece of material. Showed resulting pile of scraps to Home Economics teacher who advised me to purchase more material. Am furious, as man at store assured me that what I had would be sufficient.

8th Day: Discovered to my dismay that I had *not* been sewing front-of-skirt to back-of-skirt after all, but had been sewing it to other side of front-of-skirt. Home Economics teacher came over and watched me for a long time without saying a word. Then she left to get a drink.

9th Day: Am ready for sewing machine.

10th Day: Sewed on sewing machine. Had difficult time. Discovered finally that machine had no needle. Tried to insert needle, and something broke.

11th Day: Tried second machine with better results. Front-of-skirt is now sewed to back-of-skirt. Tried on skirt. It does not fit.

12th Day: Sewed on pocket and zipper.

13th Day: Removed pocket and zipper, as they were sewed upon inside of skirt. Hemmed skirt. Took remaining scraps of material and made little frills all over side of skirt so as to waste nothing. I shall make some man a thrifty wife!

14th Day: Project Inspection! Home Economics teacher inspected skirt. Then left room and did not return by end of period.

Expenses:

Pattern .... $	.25
Material, 3 yards	5.00
2 more yards of material	3.34
First thimble	.50
Second thimble, after losing first thimble	.25
Repairs for sewing machine	7.50
Dental work, chipped teeth	25.00
Pins, needles, bobbin, shears, etc. .	8.32
Total Expenses ......$	50.16
Cost of same skirt at store	2.50

Time spent: Two weeks

What has been learned during project: Never trust a man selling patterns and material.

Future plans: To make a blouse. I need it to go with the skirt. I confided my hopes to the Home Economics teacher, but she is planning to leave at once for California for her health, and so I shall have to wait until she returns.

Several nice things occured as a result of this story. The first, of course, was the $50 I received for it. With a portion of this I *bought* myself a skirt far nicer than any that even the most efficient seamstresses in our class had produced, and I threw the homemade mess of a skirt in the garbage.

The second was that the Home Ec teacher was so overwhelmed by the fact that someone in her class had actually sold her report to a national magazine that she changed my grade to a C. She also made me promise not to refer to her by name in the story.

The third thing was that I received my first fan letters. It seemed that half the teenage girls in the United States hated Home Ec as much as I did and were in complete sympathy with me. The letters were addressed care of the magazine and were then forwarded, and our mailbox was filled with them for weeks after the story was published. And they never altogether stopped! From then on, every once in a while, a new letter would arrive from someone who had been leafing through a back issue of *Senior Prom* in the library and had come upon my article, and just wanted me to know that I was not alone in my misery—she had flunked Home Ec too.

4

WHEN I WAS THIRTEEN I DISCOVERED DEATH. When I was fourteen, I discovered love. Not all at once, but slowly. The poems from that year are gentle and wistful—a little uncertain—filled with waiting.

Waiting
written at age 14,
published in Seventeen, *November 1949*

There was a night wind up from the river,
Slipping through the rushes, breathing on the hill.
A night cloud covered the thin moon sliver,
(And I stood waiting where the trees bent over
And the air hung heavy with the scent of clover)
And the world was still.
So still.

There was a night wind down from the meadow
Where the soft, white daisies covered the ground.
I stood waiting in the night cloud's shadow,
(Waiting for the tremor of a light foot's turning

To set the night to sudden burning)
But there was no sound.
No sound.

There was a night wind up from the gloaming.
The night cloud slipped, and the moonlight strayed
To the silent path where the dark came roaming.
(And I stood waiting, although I knew
How deep was the night between us two)
And I grew afraid.
So afraid.

Wondering
written at age 14

What would he do if I touched his hair—
Very lightly—as he passed by?
Quickly, as though I didn't care
And hadn't noticed that he was there?
Surely he wouldn't mind it much,
Just the lightest sort of touch—
And yet, for an instant, its warmth would linger
Thick and soft against my finger.

What would he think if I called his name—
All in a sudden dancing breath?
Almost a whisper—soft and low—-
Yet loudly enough so he'd hear and know;
Letting my voice leap and sing
On a name that's such a common thing
That he would think, if he thought at all,
It was somebody else I sought to call?

What would he do if I took his hand—
All of a sudden—out of the blue?
Just for a moment, and held it tight,
And dropped it quickly, the way I might
If I'd thought he was somebody else I'd known
Whose hand belonged within my own?
Just a mistake. He'd understand.
Yet, just for an instant, I'd touch his hand.

What would he do if the world stood still
And I did the things I never will?

For whom was I "waiting"? I didn't know. I could not have described the face of the prince who rode through my dreams on his snow-white steed, but I was certain that when I saw him I would know him. When I think back upon that year, it seems to have been a time of preparation, of bracing and breathing and readying myself for the turmoil of adolescence.

Besides my poetry notebooks, I began to keep a diary. The early pages contain little of interest: "I went to the movies with Roger and saw Bing Crosby in *The Bells of Saint Mary's.* . . . I stayed after school for Tri-Hi-Y meeting and then went to The Smack with the gang for a soda."

Soon, however, I began to realize that written descriptions could reinforce my visual memory, and I started inserting word pictures of things I wanted to remember.

"Our beach is a crescent," I wrote, "ending in a

sand spit at one end and rocks at the other. There is one rock shaped like a camel. It is large and smooth, and it juts out over the sea. I sit between the two humps and watch the water curl around the rocks below and slip through the crevices to fill the little green pools."

Once the words were on paper, the picture was mine. I could never forget it. Many years later I would use that very description in a novel.

I spent a lot of time with my family. Billy had now become Bill, and was more my buddy than my victim. A new magazine called *Holiday* hit the stands, and my parents were the photographers who covered assignments for them in the Southeast. On one occasion they had to do a forty-page spread of color photographs on the Florida east coast, and because it was summer, Bill and I went with them.

It was during that trip that I fell violently and abruptly in love. His name was Vic, and he was eighteen years old and first mate on a fishing boat that my parents chartered for a photo assignment off the Florida Keys.

Why try to tell about it when I can quote from my diary:

> Today I met Vic, the most wonderful guy in the world! He has curly blond hair and a beautiful build and a heart-stopping grin! We sat on the bow, and he told me all about himself. His father died when Vic was 14. His mother

handed out her children to relatives and disappeared. Vic was supposed to live with his grandparents, but they were unable to look after him, so he set out in the world by himself. He has been everywhere and seen everything! He has worked on ships out of Mexico and Cuba, and been in the Army, and worked in a Pittsburgh coal mine. . . .

Today our boat reached Dry Tortugas. There is an island with a lighthouse, and three lonely coastguardsmen who sell bootleg rum to all the boats that pass, and an old fort with a caretaker who must be a million years old. While the rest of us went ashore, Vic took our motor dingy three miles offshore and dove in forty feet of water and came back with almost seventy dollars worth of rare shells which he gave to *me!*

We ate at the coastguard lighthouse—crawfish and rice and coconut custard. Yuk! After dinner everyone sat around and sang, and I started to walk down to the beach. Vic caught up with me, and we walked along in the moonlight and poured out our hearts to each other. . . . Vic went ashore tonight and turned a 200-pound turtle who had crawled up onto the sand to lay her eggs. . . .

We had a rough sea today and ripped open a seam in the bottom of the boat. We were in bad danger, but Vic went overboard and plugged up the hole. Vic is a marvelous swimmer. He can stay underwater over two minutes, though he cannot even breathe through his nose which was injured in an ice skating accident. . . .

We docked in Key West today, and oh, how painful it was to say farewell! I gave Vic my address, and he has promised to write me, though how I will write to *him* I don't know, because there's no way to get mail when you are a wanderer. . . .
    He kissed me!!!!

So the prince came at last, and the dreamer was awakened! Just as in the fairy tale, the touch of his lips on hers did the trick. It wasn't a very long kiss (after all, poor Vic couldn't breathe through his nose), but it was magic nevertheless. I went home to wait in agony for the letters that did not come (I do believe there were a couple of postcards with "Hi, kid" scrawled across them) and to turn down dates with Roger—and to write poems about the beauty of moonlight on the ocean.

First love—first heartbreak. Who could follow in Vic's giant footprints? Yet, as with Sandy and his woodland fairy, there was no returning to innocence. I had turned the inevitable corner, and life would never be the same again.

The Corner
written at age 15
Second Place Winner in Seventeen's *Creative*
Writing Contest, January 1951

"It's not so awfully far."

Joan was painting her nails, sitting sideways on the porch swing, and Rocky was sprawled on the top step.

"We could be back by supper," he continued coaxingly, "if we took the bikes."

Joan looked up from the nail polish.

"The beach isn't any fun this late in the year," she said practically. "It's almost winter. What could we find to do on the beach after swimming weather's over? And besides, Paul might phone."

Rocky said, "Paul!" with the ultimate disgust of a twelve-year-old brother. "We used to have fun till you met that darned old Paul. You got a date with him tonight?"

Joan said, "To the Homecoming Game and the dance afterward."

She let her voice fondle the words, liking the sound of them, covering up the thin little twist of fear at the bottom of her stomach. The Homecoming Game—and dance—Paul . . .

Everything will be all right, she thought. Everything has to be all right!

"Remember last summer?" said Rocky bitterly. "You said you weren't ever going to be like that. Now you've forgotten."

"No, I haven't forgotten. I just was wrong last

summer, that's all. I didn't know about lots of things then. I was just a kid."

"You were fourteen!"

"Well, it's different now anyway. I don't know why, it just is."

She concentrated on her nails again; and her mind went back to last summer, seeing it long and lazy and golden, stretching behind her. It was the same kind of summer they'd spent every year since she could remember. She and Rocky would put on their swimming suits and ride their bicycles to the beach. They would start early in the morning with a pack lunch. Occasionally, she went with some of the girls from school, and Rocky with some of the boys who lived down the street, but usually they went together.

It was easy and comfortable to go with your brother; you never had to bother to make conversation or look attractive. Sometimes they rode the entire distance in a comfortable silence, each deep in his own thoughts. The road was bumpy, with daisies growing wild and ragged along the edges of it; and the whole day lay ahead, a lovely free summer day.

One day in particular she remembered. It was almost exactly like any other day, or had been at the time. They had left their bicycles as usual behind a dune with the basket of lunch and had run for the water. They didn't enter it slowly or gracefully, they plunged into it all at once with a great splashing.

Joan gasped at the sudden shock of the cold water about her. Then she took a deep breath and struck out. She was a good swimmer. She swam easily and strongly, her body relaxed, her strokes clean and even. Rocky could go faster, but tired more easily. He passed her, churning water like a little engine; and eventually she caught up with him again and splashed water in his face and went on farther, swimming on and on until all her strength was gone. Then she relaxed on her back in the water and let herself float in.

When she reached the beach, she sprawled out in the soft, hot sand and let the sun bake her.

Rocky came over and threw himself down beside her.

"Hot," she said.

"Uh-huh."

"You'll freckle."

"So will you."

"What makes some people freckle and other people not?"

"I don't know," said Joan. "The way their skin's made, I guess."

"Anyway, I don't blister. That would be a nasty mess, wouldn't it?"

She said, "Your crawl looks better."

"I get tired too easy."

"You just need practice."

She stretched and they lay in silence, too comfortable to make the effort that came with turning their heads to talk. The sun was almost directly above them, hot and fierce upon their backs. The sands shimmered with golden heat. The sky was the only other thing in the world; and it went on forever, thin and blue from the sea to the dunes, closing in the world and making it complete.

Suddenly there were voices.

Joan was half asleep. She felt Rocky move and lift his head.

"Hey, Joanie," he said, "it's the Brighton boy from school."

Joan said, "Who?"

"That blond guy, the one on the football team. A girl is with him."

Joan opened her eyes and blinked.

"Where?" she asked.

"Over by the far dune. They're holding hands."

That was the first time she ever really saw Paul Brighton. Oh, she had seen him at school and knew him to speak to, but she had never really looked at him. Now he stood, facing her direction, stocky and brown in lime green swimming shorts, his hair a shocking splash of yellow against his dark skin.

He met her eyes and smiled and raised his hand in casual greeting before turning back to the girl at his side.

"He waved at you!" exclaimed Rocky.

Joan smiled. "The fatal charm. You have an irresistible sister."

"Who's the gal?"

"Nancy Trousdale. Nice."

"Pretty," observed Rocky.

"Uh-huh."

She relaxed again, burying her face in the sand, not particularly caring about Paul or Nancy or anyone else. The sun was a gigantic force, boring its way into her, becoming part of her. If she could just let herself lie still enough, and let her mind haze with sleep, she would become part of the sun.

Rocky said, "They're walking off. He's got a car parked over near our bikes. He's still holding her hand. She looks like she likes it." He reached over and touched her shoulder "Joanie?"

"Yes."

His voice was suddenly worried. "You won't ever be like that, will you? You won't get all silly and dopey about some guy and hold hands with him and stuff?"

Joan said, "No, of course not."

"But I'm not joking. I mean, honest, you won't, will you?"

Joan said, "I'm not joking either." She sat up. "Come on, Rocky," she said suddenly, "let's take a dip before lunch."

The water was warmer the second time than it had been at first. Joan washed the sand off and came out again. She stood on the beach, watching Rocky's head as it bobbed about, a black dot against the silver of the water. There was a slight wind, blowing along the beach and stirring the sand into little puffs that rose and fell back in waves. The wind was cold when it hit her wet suit.

She stood there, feeling the heat of the sun on her head and the cold of the wind against her body, knowing the delicious tiredness in her arms and legs, secure in the strength of her slim body. She felt apart from everyone and everything in the world, a being that had no place in a world of ordinary people like her mother and father and Nancy and

Paul and the teachers at school. Even a little apart from Rocky.

"I am Joan!" she whispered to the wind and to the beach and to the sun. "I am Joan! I am Joan!"

She began to run, and in a moment Rocky had caught up with her and was running beside her, and it turned into a race for the dunes and picnic basket.

That seemed so long ago.

Joan inspected the drying fingernails and leaned back in the porch swing. There was still the touch of fear at the bottom of her stomach, the funny, empty feeling that wouldn't go away. But it would have to go away. The Homecoming Game—the dance—Paul!

Half her mind listened for the telephone, and the other half drifted back, taking thoughts at random and dwelling upon them so she would not have time to let the fear feeling get hold of her.

The summer was long and lovely, like every other summer. It was like a straight smooth road, coming from one direction; and the autumn was like another road, entirely different, coming from somewhere else. Somewhere the two roads joined and made a corner. Somewhere there had been a place to stand from which she could choose either direction she wished. But the corner had been passed without her even knowing that it was there; and, try as she would, she couldn't quite recall where the corner had been or when she had turned it.

School began, with the clamor of voices and the crash of lockers and the smell of books. The first few days were crowded with learning a locker combination, meeting new teachers, and starting new classes.

It wasn't till the second week that she met Paul.

He passed her in the hall, walking along with his arms loaded with books. He smiled and nodded and was lost in the crowd.

Joan watched the back of his head disappear among the dozens of other heads that bobbed back and forth between classrooms, and thought suddenly that he was very handsome, perhaps the handsomest boy in school. The next moment she wondered where Nancy was and why she wasn't with him.

For some strange reason, she kept thinking of him again and again. During history class, while she was studying her chemistry notes, while the Latin translation lay staring from the page before her, she kept seeing Paul. Paul without Nancy.

Three days later she saw him again. She not only saw him, she found him walking beside her and carrying her books as she left school. She didn't quite know how it happened, only she was glad that it had.

"Your freckles are fading," he told her observingly.

"Second year Latin is enough to fade anything," she answered. "But they'll be back next summer, don't worry."

"I know," he said. "I saw you acquiring them, remember?"

She blushed. "I remember. I'm surprised that you do."

"Why wouldn't I? It's not every day you see a

pretty girl lying on the beach beside her little brother."

"At least," Joan said pointedly, "it *was* my little brother," and she could have bitten her tongue off a moment after she said it.

"Oh," said Paul. "You mean, Nancy," and he frowned. "That's over and done with. Just a summer romance. You know how it is."

"Yes," said Joan. "Of course, I know." She didn't know in the least, but she felt happy that it was over and that Paul did not seem particularly sorry. She passed some of her friends and waved at them. She was very conscious of Paul walking beside her. She watched the girls' faces with a thrill of pleasure.

That was only the first time. He walked home with her the next day and the day after that, and by the end of the week it had become a regular thing. He took her to the movies Friday night, and roller skating Saturday. It was something she had never known before—having a good-looking boy's face a few inches above her own, and warm, boyish laughter after all her jokes, and a ready car to take her places, and a ready arm to open a door or carry books or guide her safely across the street. She was in a daze about how it had originated. Two weeks ago she would never have thought of such a thing and then, suddenly, it was almost as though it had been there always.

"That's the way things like this happen, I guess," she said to Rocky. "They just happen for no reason. But—but—oh, Rocky, Paul's so wonderful!"

Rocky said, "I don't like him. I think he's a dope."

But Joan could not make herself care very much what he thought, because the next week was a dance. The first football game of the season—and the dance after it—and she went with Paul.

In thinking back, there was no clear-cut picture of the way the dance had been. It all fell into a rosy blur of music and dancers swaying to the rhythm and little tables with flowers and gay, colored streamers.

The ride home in Paul's car was a blur too, sweet and undefinably wonderful. There had been a moon. And he had kissed her. Even the kiss was hard to remember. It didn't stand out as a shining token, the way a first kiss is supposed to. He had kissed her a great deal afterward, and all the times got mixed up together. But she would always remember that he *had* kissed her, and she had worn flowers in her hair, and the seat had smelled of leather.

Perhaps, thought Joan, that was the corner. Yes, I do believe that was it.

The telephone rang.

Rocky jerked to a sitting position on the step.

"That's probably him," he remarked impatiently. "Why don't you go answer it?"

Joan clenched her hands in her lap until they hurt. I don't want it to be Paul, she thought wildly. Oh, please don't make it be Paul!

The phone rang again.

There was the sound of the receiver being lifted and then her mother's muffled voice. The voice rose in a greeting, responded again and fell into an easy conversation.

Joan felt an immense wave of relief.

"It's for Mother," she said.

"Look," said Rocky, "if you don't want to talk to him, why do you hang around? We could take the bikes and go to the beach and be back in time to eat. Of course we couldn't swim this late in the year, but that doesn't matter. We can ride down and fool around and come back like we always used to do. Golly, Joanie, what's wrong with you? We used to always do things like that."

Joan said, "I don't want him to call, but if he does I want to be here. Can't you understand?"

Rocky said, "No. I think you're dopey as you can be."

He got up and sauntered around the side of the house.

"I guess I'll get my bike," he said, "and go by myself. I guess I can go by myself as good as not."

From the living room there came the click of the receiver being hung up.

Joan thought, Maybe I shouldn't have done it. know I shouldn't have. It's not the kind of thing girl does, but I just couldn't see it fall apart and no do anything. I had to try! Oh, please don't let him phone and make some excuse and call it off! Give me this one more chance! Please!

There was no reason for its having cooled off except that it had. There was nothing to point at and say, "What's wrong? What's the matter?" It had just slipped away quietly, in the same way it had sprung up. Joan couldn't understand it. In school, he was distant but polite. He simply wasn't around much

He smiled in a friendly way when he saw her, but he seldom found time to see her. He had football practice after school every afternoon, so he didn't walk her home anymore, and she walked with a group of girls. For years she had walked with girls and not minded at all; but now she was very conscious that they weren't Paul, and she minded very much.

There hadn't been any dates for a long time. Paul was always busy—always going somewhere, always doing something that did not include her.

The Homecoming Dance was the big dance of the season. It followed the biggest game.

Joan thought, He's bound to ask me! He *must* ask me!

But the days slipped by and he didn't. And then there was only one day left before the dance, and it was too late for him possibly to think of asking her.

That afternoon on her way out of school, Joan passed his locker. It was open, and Paul was standing in front of it, stuffing in a pair of gym shoes and a skivvy shirt.

Joan stopped.

"Paul?"

He raised his head and nodded.

"Hi."

"Walking home?"

"Nope. Football. You know that."

Joan said, "Sure." She took a deep breath. "Paul, is something wrong?"

He looked at her sharply. "No, of course not.

Nothing's wrong. It's just that—oh, you know how it is."

"No," said Joan. "I don't know how it is. I—that is—the Homecoming Dance is tomorrow night, Paul."

She knew she shouldn't have said it. She should have let him call it the way he wanted it to be. But somehow she couldn't. Not like this. Not without even having made an effort to save it, when there was no reason for its being this way.

She said, "Are we going, Paul?"

He closed the locker.

He said, "I don't know, Joanie. I don't—"

"It's the big dance of the year! Or—" Suddenly the thought came to her, "Or are you taking somebody else? Mona or Dolores or—or Nancy?"

"No," he said. "I'm not taking anybody else. It's not that. It's—well, okay. We'll go."

The world shone suddenly, wonderful and clear. She had won! One night was all she needed—one magic night like that first dance—and everything would be safe again. She knew it would.

"I'll be at the game, Paul, to watch you play. And I'll meet you at the door to the locker room afterward."

"All right," he said. "I guess that'll be okay."

It had been fine, perfect! Until that fear began to gnaw.

She thought, I know I shouldn't have made him say he would take me. But it was the only way! And I know I can bring it all back again if I have tonight.

Please let me have tonight! Please don't let him call it off!

Her fingernails were dry.

The phone rang.

There was a pause, and then her mother's voice said, "Joan!"

Joan took a deep breath and went into the house and picked up the receiver.

"Hello?"

"Hello. This is Paul."

His voice was the voice of a very little boy, carefully repeating a memorized speech.

"Hello, Paul."

Suddenly it didn't matter anymore. Whether they went or not didn't matter. Down deep inside she had known all along that there would not be another magic night. And now she didn't even care.

"Look, Joanie, I'm sorry, but I won't be able to take you to the dance tonight. My dad says I've got to get the car in early, right after the game. He wants it for something."

She thought, We could use the bus! But she didn't say it.

"I'll probably see you at the game," he went on. "I'll look for you in the stands. I'll probably see you there. Okay?"

"Yes," said Joan, "that's all right. That's all right, Paul."

She hung up the receiver and came back to the porch. Strangely enough there was no great bitterness or hurt. There was just numbness. She was over. The way Nancy had been over. A summer romance more or less—an autumn romance—what did they matter?

She thought of the summer, the long golden summer stretching behind her, free of twisting little jealousies and fears, free of sudden sweet joy, free of agonizing moments of heartbreak that come so easily at fifteen and last such a short time and yet fill the world so completely while they last. Only she and Rocky, swimming and laughing and lying in the sand with the strong, hot sun beating down upon them the summer long.

She thought, I can go now and still catch up with Rocky before he reaches the dunes. I can take my bike and head him off by going through the short cut. It can be the same as it was last summer! It can be—

She was halfway down the steps before she stopped, knowing that it *couldn't* be the same. They could do the same things again, but she would no longer be "Joan." She would be "Joan, the girl Pat kissed." That would never be the same. And she and Rocky would not be the same, because between them would be the thin line that separates a child from a person who has passed childhood and is growing up. And all the while there would be an emptiness that would not go away.

Once you're around the corner, she thought, you can't go back. You can't ever go back again. No matter how much you want to, there isn't any way to go back. Only ahead.

Suddenly, she began to cry—silent, scared crying

—a way she had never cried before. It wasn't for Paul. There would be other Pauls. But for something rather precious that had slipped away from her and been left behind—and lost forever—around the corner. On the other street.

WAS "THE CORNER" ABOUT VIC?

No, of course not. I did write stories about him, but they were rejected.

"He isn't believable," one editor wrote me. "At age eighteen he's been in the Army? Worked in a coal mine? Been first mate on half a dozen ships?"

"But, it's all true!" I told her.

"The words 'true' and 'believable' are not synonymous," the editor responded. "Something may really have happened, but if it is not something our readers can accept, then for them it remains 'impossible.' If they *did* believe in Vic, they wouldn't be able to relate to him. He would seem like somebody from another planet. The boys our readers fall in love with are juniors and seniors in high school."

So I laid Vic to rest in the pages of my diary with a eulogy of poetry. Most of those poems are tributes to his God-like build and curly hair, but one takes things a bit farther:

The Quiet Wife
written at age 15

She used to know a lowly man;
He had a boat tied in the bay.
They used to laugh a lot and sing
Such silly songs, and everything
We elders warned or tried to say
She tossed aside. They used to go
A-walking hand in hand at night
Along the shore. We let her know
How people talked. She didn't care.
She said his eyes were soft and gray
And that the dampness curled his hair.

You wouldn't know it now, but she
Was always such a pretty child.
(She's been a good daughter to me
Since she and my son, Bill, were wed.)
You'd never think she once was wild.

She used to laugh at what we said
About this man she used to know.
He caught her fishes in a net
At night by moonlight. Where they'd go
We couldn't ever make her say,
But she'd come home all drenching wet,
Her soft hair limp with salty spray.

She used to talk a lot. My Bill
Says that she is a model wife,

So thoughtful, kind, and keeps so still
You scarce would know that she was there.

She used to know a lowly man,
Until one night he went away.
She came a-weeping home at dawn.
Where he had gone she'd never say.
She only said that he was gone,
His boat was gone from out the bay.

Now she and Bill are quite content,
Except she is so very still.
Sometimes I wonder where he went.
I see her turn her eyes toward Bill
And quickly turn and look away.
She used to know a lowly man
When she was young and slim and gay.

I wonder where he is today?

Looking back, I find that poem interesting. A
though it is about a girl in love, it is not written fro
her viewpoint. I had finally reached a point as
writer where I could step back from my subject an
view it through someone else's eyes. That ability
detach and move slightly away from what you a
writing is not easily developed, but it is necessar
Sometimes I feel that I am two people in one, with
part of me living each experience and another pa
observing.

"My heart is breaking!" Part One may cry.

"This will be a challenge," Part Two will respond coolly. "How am I going to show how upset this woman is without making her appear foolish?"

A second interesting thing about this poem is that although I was writing it from the viewpoint of the girl's mother-in-law, every man who has ever read it—my father, my English teacher, the editor of this book—assumed that the viewpoint character was the father-in-law. Because there is no indication of the sex of the observer, each reader interprets the poem in the way that he or she can best relate to it.

By writing Vic out of my system, I was able to unblock and move on to the next stage of development. I was able to write "The Corner." Although the story is not about Vic at all, I could not have written it if I had not gone through that first romance. The average reader of teen magazines might not have found Vic believable, but she could relate to love and loss in a high school setting. "Paul" I invented. He was Vic's cardboard substitute. "Joan" was myself, and my brother was "Rocky." The story's theme was straight from "The Fairy in the Woods": that growing up is painful and that the uncomplicated magic of childhood, once lost, can never be regained.

I entered "The Corner" in *Seventeen*'s Creative Writing Contest, and it placed second. That $200 award money was the most I had ever received. With this windfall, plus what was in my savings account as a result of previous sales, I bought a secondhand Jeep.

Now I had wheels.

I also still had Roger. Dear, faithful Roger had waited patiently through the Vic fiasco in hopes that I would come to my senses and realize that true love had been there right under my nose all the time.

Roger took me to dances, and at those dances I met Don and Arnold and Tom and Fenton and David and Lee and Bob and Barry.

By the time I turned sixteen, I was having a very good time indeed.

I never fell in love with Roger, but I was grateful for his adoration, even when I became too busy to go out with him. I wrote a story about him which, to my credit, I wasn't crass enough to submit to a magazine at that time. I tucked it away in a drawer, and many years later, when both Roger and I were married (to different people), and my young husband was in law school, and a baby was coming, I took it out and sold it. I felt a little guilty, but I reassured myself that somebody as nice as Roger wouldn't hold it against me. Besides, he'd never know.

A Gift from Roger
written at age 16,
published in American Girl, *September 1960*

I met Roger in the orthodontist's office. Now I think back on it, that might have been what put the damper on our whole relationship. Perhaps in my subconscious mind I connected him with wires and mouth rinses and wads of cotton. My little brother Billy and I were sitting quietly in the waiting room, looking at magazines and waiting to have our braces tightened, when Roger walked over and said, "Hi."

"Hi," I said absentmindedly. I was reading a very good story.

"I—I noticed you here last week," Roger said hesitantly. "I'm Roger Cunningham. I was here last week too."

"Oh." This time I looked up and almost wished I hadn't bothered. Roger was an unimpressive boy, tall and thin and blond. I liked boys to have dark, curly hair and broad shoulders.

"I'm Laurie Nolan," I said.

"Yes," said Roger eagerly. "I know. I've seen you at school. Your locker number is seventy-eight. Mine's eighty-nine. It's eleven down from yours."

"Yes," I agreed, doing some hasty arithmetic in my head, "I suppose it must be." At this point the nurse motioned that Dr. Thomas was ready for me, so I said, "So long," and walked away—never expecting to see Roger again. By the time we reached home I had completely forgotten him.

Billy hadn't. "A boy talked to Laurie in the dentist's office," he reported at the dinner table. "He talked to her a long time. He even knew her locker number."

"Really?" Mother's face brightened with interest. "How very nice! Who was he, Laurie?"

"Roger Something-or-Other," I told her.

"You mean you don't even know his last name?"

"He said it, but I didn't pay any attention." I squirmed self-consciously. "I was reading a magazine."

"Oh, honey, for goodness' sake," Mother began, but Daddy gave her a stern look and shook his head.

"Let's not make a federal case of this, dear. Laurie isn't interested in boys yet. Lots of fourteen-year-old girls aren't interested in boys."

"But if she made a little effort—" Mother began again, and then with a despairing little shrug she let the matter drop.

That's the way it was with Mother and Daddy. Each one understood me a little, but not about the same things. And each of them was in his or her own way wrong.

Daddy was wrong when he said I was not interested in boys. I was. Not in boys in general; in one certain boy—Joe Reigle.

To tell you how I felt about Joe, I'll have to tell you first that he had never looked at me. Not ever. We were in the same English class and he sat only two seats ahead of me, so I could spend the whole hour staring at the back of his neck. It was a very tan neck because he was athletic and spent a lot of time out-of-doors. He wore bright colored sports shirts that made him look even more tanned and his curly hair look even blacker than it really was. Once in a while I had a front view of him when he turned around to speak to Cindy Gilbret who sat directly behind him.

I don't know when I first began to notice Joe. It

just seemed to happen. I knew from the very beginning that he belonged exclusively to Cindy Gilbret, but when a crowd of boys walked past, Joe would be the only one I saw. When he spoke—even to Cindy in a whisper—his would be the voice I heard above all the other voices. He had a low voice, lower than any of the other boys, and a slow, amused way of talking. He had a nice laugh too—a strong, happy laugh.

So Daddy was wrong. I did care about boys, but I would have died before admitting it to anyone because, you see, Mother was wrong too. She seemed to think that all I had to do was to want boys to like me and they would. If I had told her about Joe and that he had been in a class with me all year and still did not know I existed, she would have been sure there was something wrong with him. She was my mother, and with that odd, devoted blindness that mothers seem to have, she thought I was pretty.

Pretty! Sometimes I said the word very softly to myself when I was looking in the mirror. How far from pretty I was! I had the kind of face people look right through without seeing. My hair was straight and hair-colored—that mousy, in-between shade that people never quite know what to call. I had a nose that was a bit too short and a mouth a bit too big and skin that broke out every time I looked at a chocolate bar. When I walked I bumped into things, and when I smiled my braces flashed in the sunlight like a field of artillery. I couldn't even talk entertainingly. At home I could come out with all sorts of sparkling remarks, but the minute a boy stood in front of me, my tongue froze and I couldn't make an intelligent comment. I knew with a terrible inner certainty that no boy in the world would ever look at me twice, and there was no sense making a fool of myself by trying to attract one.

Which is why I was so completely unprepared when the phone rang and Daddy, who went to answer it, came back to the dinner table and said, "It's for Laurie. It's a boy." He sounded surprised.

"Hello, Laurie?" The voice on the phone was strained and nervous. "This is Roger. Roger Cunningham from the dentist's office. Remember?"

"Yes," I said blankly. Why in the world would he be calling me? "How are you, Roger?"

"Fine." The voice wavered slightly. "I thought —that is, I was wondering—are you going to the Student Council Dance next weekend?"

"No," I said.

"Well, would you like to go?"

"You mean, with you?" I could not believe I had heard him correctly.

"Yes."

"All right," I said.

I was so stunned I could hardly replace the receiver. When I got back to the table, I found my family eagerly awaiting me.

"It's Cunningham," I told them. "That's his last name—Cunningham. And he's asked me to the Student Council Dance."

The Student Council Dance! I repeated the words to myself as I was lying in bed that night. I was going to a dance! They were words I had never said before. I could hardly believe I was saying them. I was going to a dance! Not with Joe; the gates of heaven had not opened to present me with Joe. But even if he weren't Joe, Roger was a *boy* and he *had* asked me to a dance!

The next day in English class I leaned forward and whispered to Cindy Gilbret, "What are you wearing to the dance Saturday?"

"My red taffeta," she said, turning to me with interest. "Are you going too?"

I nodded as though it were a matter of no importance. "I thought I might."

"Who's taking you?" asked Cindy.

"His name's Roger Cunningham," I said. "You probably don't know him."

But she surprised me. "Roger Cunningham? Sure, I know Roger. He and Joe are on the Student Council together." There was a note of respect in her voice. "He's a senior, isn't he?"

"I don't know," I said. There was a good deal of prestige connected with dating a senior in our high school.

"I'm sure he is," said Cindy.

Cindy was not the quiet type; by noon all the girls in our class knew that a senior had invited me to the Student Council Dance. Several of them spoke to me about it in the cafeteria. The most popular ones asked me what I was wearing and what table we were reserving, and a lot of other friendly little details. The girls who had not been invited treated me with awed respect.

At home, my mother was mad with excitement.

She took the month's household money and rushed me from store to store, recklessly spending it. We bought a gorgeous blue dress with a swirling skirt, shoes with pointed heels, stunning earrings made like little gold chains, and an evening bag.

"Just think," Mother said delightedly, "your very first date! Aren't you terribly, terribly excited?"

"I guess so," I said. I thought about it a moment. I should be excited. I really wanted to be excited. But somehow when I thought about Roger no light went on inside me, no chills ran up my spine. He just drooped there in my mind, and all I could think about was the orthodontist's office and the taste of mouthwash.

Maybe you're remembering him wrong, I told myself. After all, you've talked to him just once. Maybe when you know him you'll like him as much as you do Joe.

I kept saying it to myself, but I never really believed it. And when I caught my next glimpse of Roger, all dressed up and holding a corsage box in his hand, I knew it was hopeless. He was just as tall and just as thin and just as blond as ever, and I still liked dark-haired boys.

"I hope you don't mind walking," he told me when we had finally escaped my parents' feverish good-byes and made it down the steps to the street. "I—I don't have my driver's license yet."

"I don't mind at all," I said. I noticed he was twisting his hands around in his pockets and biting his lip and doing all sorts of odd little things. Good heavens, I thought, the truth of the matter dawning upon me, he's nervous! He's nervous because of me! With that thought came another realization. If he's nervous, it means he cares what I think of him. It means—it was unbelievable—it means he really likes me! He might even feel about me the way I do about Joe!

Poor Roger, I thought pityingly. After a while I noticed he wasn't talking. Probably, I thought, he doesn't know what to say. I should do something to make him more comfortable.

"What do you like to do?" I asked to break the silence. It was the kind of question I had read about in "how-to-be-popular" articles, but I had never been able to blurt it out before.

Roger's face brightened in relief.

"I raise tropical fish," he told me. "I have an aquarium five feet long with its own temperature regulator. It's divided into three different compartments—" He was so enthusiastic, he didn't even stammer. The subject supplied conversation all the way to the dance.

The dance itself was really wonderful. The gym was decorated in gold and purple, our school colors. There were crepe-paper streamers and big bunches of balloons hanging from the ceiling. There were mobs of people. Some of them I didn't know but some of them I did. All the girls from my class smiled and waved at me. It was as though I had been promoted suddenly to their pretty, popular group. Being here with a senior, even a senior like Roger, was enough to do it. Roger was not a good dancer— his hands were damp and sticky and he counted out loud—but he was a boy and he had taken me to a dance. That was the important thing.

"You're a wonderful dancer," he told me as we staggered across the floor.

"You're easy to follow," I answered.

This was true enough, as Roger's dancing consisted of two steps in one direction followed by two steps in the other. In his right hand he clutched the back of my dress, and with his left he kept a viselike grip on my fingers. It was impossible to do anything but follow him.

At intermission we found a table and Roger got some punch. On the far side of the dance floor I saw Cindy Gilbret, stunning in her red taffeta. I tried to see who was with her.

"What are you doing?" Roger asked curiously as I teetered on the edge of my chair.

"I'm just trying to see what color Cindy Gilbret's dress is," I told him.

"It's red," Roger said without interest. It was the first time I had ever seen a boy show lack of interest in Cindy. "Laurie, I have to tell you something."

"Yes, Roger?" I tore my eyes away from Cindy. Her escort was still hidden behind a post. "What is it?"

"I just want you to know," Roger said awkwardly, "that I—well, I didn't just happen to meet you at the orthodontist's office the other day. I—I made my appointment for that day because I knew you were going to be there."

"You did?" I said in surprise. "How did you know that?"

"I asked the receptionist." His face was red with embarrassment. "I called her and asked her. I noticed you at school at the very beginning of the year, and I'd been wanting to meet you, but every time I saw you in the hall I couldn't think of anything to say. I'm telling you all this," he said, swallowing hard, "because I don't want you to think I'm the kind of guy who just sees a girl for the first time and calls her right up for a date. I mean, I want you to know that—that I've been thinking about calling you—for months and months."

His voice faded miserably off.

I said, "I'm glad you did call me, Roger."

"Gee, are you really?" His whole face lighted up with pleasure. "Say, there's the orchestra again. Shall we dance?"

This time as we staggered back and forth on the dance floor, Cindy Gilbret swept by in the arms of her escort. She smiled and waved, and although I got only a rear view of her date, the back of his neck was not tan.

If Joe didn't bring Cindy, I thought, then who—

And then I saw him. He was standing by himself on the edge of the dance floor. He looked very handsome in his navy blue suit with his black hair slicked back and already beginning to curl forward again. It was odd to see him by himself like that. At school he almost always had a circle of friends about him. He was looking at the dancers, and there was a funny expression of loss on his face.

He's looking for Cindy, I thought at once. Then as we lurched in his direction and his eyes swept across

73

us, I did something I had never had the nerve to do before. I smiled at him. His eyes focused on me and he looked puzzled, as though trying to remember who I was. And then, to my complete amazement, he walked across the floor and put his hand on Roger's shoulder.

"Rog, old boy," he said in that low voice of his, "may I cut in?"

So suddenly that I could not believe it, his arm was around me and we were dancing! Dancing with Joe Riegle! I had dreamed about it, of course. Sometimes at night before I went to sleep I would lie in bed and imagine myself dancing with Joe, with his arm around me and his face looking down into mine. Always in those dreams I knew exactly what to say—that certain special combination of words to make his face brighten with interest. Now I could think of nothing.

"I know you," he said, "don't I?"

I said, "I'm Laurie Nolan. I sit two behind you in English class."

"Oh, sure," he said politely. "I'm no good at remembering people. Are you Roger's steady?"

"Oh, no," I told him hastily. "I'm just here with him tonight."

"Smart girl." There was a touch of bitterness in his voice. "Don't tie yourself up steady; it gives you too big a jolt when you break off. Cindy and I had our final blowup last night."

I struggled to keep elation from my voice. "I'm sorry."

"It had been coming for some time, I guess," he said stiffly. "It didn't take her too long to get another date, I see. She was probably holding him in reserve, waiting to see which of us she preferred to go with."

His jaw tightened and he fell into silence. The dance was nearly over. In a moment the music would stop and he would return me to Roger and probably never look at me again. I had to say something—something to interest him—anything—

In desperation I reached back in my mind for the words I had used with Roger earlier that night. "What do you like to do?"

"What do I like to do?" he repeated. "Why, I like to do a lot of things. I play football, I go hunting, I go skiing, I bowl—"

"You bowl?" I caught quickly at the one interest with which I was familiar. I had bowled occasionally with my brother Billy. "Do you do a lot of bowling?"

"Sometimes on Saturday nights. At least, I used to, with Cindy." But this time when he said "Cindy" it was just part of a sentence. "Do you bowl too?"

"I'm pretty terrible, but I enjoy it," I said.

"We'll have to go sometime. Maybe next week-end."

The music stopped and the words echoed loud in the sudden silence. Had he said them? Had he actually said them! Could Joe Reigle possibly be asking me for a date?

No, I thought, no. Things like this don't happen. I've misunderstood him.

We were walking back toward the table where

Roger was waiting. Joe presented me to him with a friendly nod. "Thanks for letting me cut, Rog. Thanks for the dance, Laurie. I'll give you a call sometime next week."

"Fine," I murmured and fell into a chair.

But I did not have time to recover my composure, for Roger was already on his feet. "Come on, let's start dancing before somebody else comes over to ask you!" He sounded as though at any moment a wild stampede might start in my direction.

The rest of the evening passed quickly in a kind of dreamy haze. I remember only a blur of music and dancing couples, and then finally the lights went dim and bright again as the orchestra ended with "Good Night, Ladies." Everyone began to mill around, collecting coats. Then we were outside and there was a moon which cast patterns of light and shadow on the sidewalk and it was still a dream. Joe had danced with me. He was going to telephone me next week. This time next Saturday I might be walking along this very sidewalk with *Joe!*

Roger's hand closed over mine. It was a clammy hand but I obligingly held it. We walked in silence. I pretended it was Joe beside me and that this was Joe's hand, and immediately it became a lot more pleasant to hold. I kept my eyes straight ahead, and the boy beside me had black, curly hair and broad shoulders. The night was soft with magic, and I carried my dream with me all the way home.

Then it was time to say good night, and of course the boy with me was only Roger. We stood there by the porch steps, a little unsure how to act with each other. I wondered if I should invite Roger in. It was what girls did in books, but I could not imagine what I would do with him once I got him inside; and there would be the problem of getting him out again.

So I merely said, "This has been a very nice evening, Roger."

"Did you have a good time?" There was a hopeful croak in his voice. "Really?"

"A lovely time," I said, thinking of Joe. "The nicest time I've ever had."

"Gee, I'm glad," Roger said earnestly. "I did too. I—I—look, Laurie—" His voice faded out and came in strong again. "Look, could you—I mean, well, what about doing something next Saturday? Going to a movie or something?"

"I'm sorry," I said. "I have plans for next weekend."

"Oh." Roger was silent a moment and then he said, "I guess I should have known you'd be dated up. I mean, a girl as pretty as you are—"

I stared at him. "What?"

"A girl as pretty as you are," he repeated. "I should have known—there must be lots of guys—I just hoped—maybe—"

He turned a little, and I could see his face in the moonlight, and there was a look there I had seen on the faces of boys before, boys who gazed at girls like Cindy Gilbret, a kind of helpless, worshipful, puppy-dog expression. My goodness, I thought numbly, is this for me? Is this look for me? The words he had spoken seemed to echo all around us— "I should have known—a girl as pretty as you are—"

He had said I was pretty! Suddenly, amazingly, I believed it, this thing that Mother had been telling me for years. I believed it because Roger believed it! I was not, as I had always believed, a dull, uninteresting, homely, tongue-tied little nothing. I had whatever it was that made boys fall for girls! I must have it, because Roger was a boy and Roger thought I was wonderful!

"Roger." I said his name softly. I knew even as I said it that never, never, would I find it romantic. Never, no matter how hard I tried, would I talk myself into feeling for Roger what I felt for Joe. Roger to me would always be the orthodontist's office, damp hands, and an aquarium of tropical fish. But Roger tonight had given me something no one else ever had, something I would have always, and there was only one thing I could give him in return.

"Roger," I said, "about Saturday night—I can change my plans. I would like very much to go to the movies with you."

"Gee!" There was wonder in his voice. "You really mean it?"

"I'll see you at school on Monday," I said, "and we'll settle the details."

There was a happiness inside me—a warm, glowing sureness that I had never known before. If Joe called about Saturday, I would tell him the truth, that I already had a date, and ask him to call another tıme. And he *would* call again—I knew it—because I was worth calling. If one boy cared about me, there would be others! There were sure to be others!

"Good night, Roger," I said, and slowly and gracefully, as beautiful as any Cindy Gilbret, I walked into the house.

6

JOE REIGLE, IN "A GIFT FROM ROGER," was in real life a boy named Don. I won't bother describing him, since I've already described Joe. Suffice to say, he was extremely handsome, and the heroines of all the stories I wrote during that period were in love with boys who looked exactly like him.

Don was not in love with me, but he did like my Jeep. Since he himself did not have a car, he was limited in the girls he could date; they either had to live within walking distance of his home or have their own means of transportation. Don would wait until Friday night, and then, if nothing more interesting turned up to occupy his time, he would call and invite me to chauffeur him to the movies.

I spent a good many Friday evenings sitting by that phone.

I have many odes to Don in my poetry notebook, but few are as honest as this one:

Song of Frustration
written at age 16,
published in Seventeen, *1951*

Roger will call at 8:15,
This I know for a fact.
I know exactly what Roger will say
And just how Roger will act.
Roger's the sweetest lad in town,
He thinks of me night and day. . . .
(But maybe—maybe—Don will call!
Please, dear heaven, that Don should call!
If he happens to think of it, Don might call,
And I mustn't be away.)

Roger will call at 8:15,
Never a moment late.
Roger is thoughtful and fine and sweet,
Really a perfect date.
There's always Roger who's awfully nice,
(But if I sit home alone
Maybe—maybe—Don will call!
If there's nothing better he just might call,
And please, dear heaven, if he should call,
I have to be near the phone!)

Roger will call at 8:15
As he always has before,
But, if I leave it, the phone will ring
The moment I've shut the door.

And so, I guess, I'll stay at home
And read a while in bed. . . .
(And wait and wait for Don to call,
And tell myself, "He still might *call!")*

Though I know damned well he'll never call,
And I wish
      that
        I
          were
            dead!

When the poem came out in *Seventeen,* the boys'
names were changed to "Johnny" and "Steve" and
quick-eyed editors changed "I know damned well"
to "I know so well." To protect Roger's feelings and
keep from supercharging Don's ego, I was in favor
of the first alteration, but I was very upset by the
second. I felt that the ending of the poem needed
that extra punch.

When I wrote the editor about this, I was stunned
to discover that I didn't have any say-so.

"It is not our policy to publish profanity," she told
me. "Our advertisers wouldn't approve." She also
pointed out that, since her magazine had purchased
my poem, it now belonged to them, and they could
do anything with it they chose. I had created a
product and sold it, and it was no longer mine.

"If it had been a dress," the editor said, "even
though you had designed and sewed it, you wouldn't

feel you had the right to object if the buyer replaced the buttons."

I had to admit that what she said made sense. At the same time, I didn't like it. My poems and stories were *not* dresses. Dresses were made from store-bought material. The fabric for my writing was woven from my own thoughts and emotions. It was part of *me!*

"What can I do?" I asked Mother. "I don't want my work to be hacked up by strangers."

"Then don't offer it for sale," she said reasonably.

"But I want it published!"

"It's your choice," Mother said. "Either you're a professional or you're not. Nobody is forcing you to submit to magazines. There are plenty of people who enjoy writing just for the fun of putting thoughts on paper."

I was not such a person. I considered writing communication. I wanted my stories to be *read*. The money was unimportant. In truth, I didn't even spend it. I had never gotten much pleasure out of buying things. I had my car and my typewriter, and except for the gas and ribbons necessary to keep them going, there wasn't anything I especially wanted. But I had tasted the power that comes with knowing that you can affect the lives of others, and I wasn't about to give that up by hiding my stories in bureau drawers.

So, I decided to accept the situation. I decided, also, to find out as much as I could about writing as a profession. I had never realized that advertisers had control over what a magazine printed. I had not thought about such things as "rights." Now, suddenly, it came home to me that I didn't know a thing about the business end of the career I had chosen for myself, and I started reading everything I could find on the subject.

Meanwhile, Don fell in love with a girl named Janet, and I fell in love with a boy named Arnold.

Arnold was not handsome, as Don was. He was short, with a stocky build and irregular features. What he did have was intensity and brilliance. I have no idea what his IQ was. I wouldn't try to guess. I only know that I was so outdistanced that it was like being a candle next to a skyrocket. A full year younger than I, he had read all the classics, studied all the philosophers, absorbed every period of history, and memorized the music of a hundred composers. He gave concerts on piano, clarinet and saxophone, playing his own compositions.

During the year his parents permitted him to attend public school, Arnold and I were constant companions, and for the first time I had a contemporary I could really talk to. With my other friends, I represented my writing as a "sort of hobby," on a par with tennis or tap dancing. Since I wrote under a pen name, when they came across my stories in magazines, they seldom realized that I had written them. I was terrified of being considered "weird" and "different" and not a regular part of the gang.

With Arnold I was secure, because he was "differ-ent" too. We clicked into place like two halves of a unit. We talked. We argued. We competed.

Above all, we tried to impress each other.

I never wrote *about* Arnold except in my diary. I could not take that necessary step backward to look at him objectively. The result of his influence was that everything I wrote during that period was for his benefit.

One afternoon he took me (via my Jeep, of course) to hear a pianist named Alex Templeton. It was my first exposure to classical piano, and to prove to Arnold that I appreciated the experience, I wrote a poem about it.

Sunday Afternoon Piano Concert
written at age 16

The piano is only a dead black box
Until he sits down and presses his fingers upon the keys,
And then beneath his touch it becomes a living thing;
Softly, softly, a dawn wind up from the river,
Coolness and mist and stars.
Softly the light, strong hands fondle the keys
And bring the mists in from the river
And bring the stars down from the sky;
Faster and faster, until the music rises
To a glittering cascade of silver,
Pouring forth across the afternoon,
Building Debussy's castles into the sky
And tumbling them again into the sea,

Filling the room with the roar of the sea
And the walls of castles sinking beneath the waves.

People turn and look at each other and look away.

A boy in the front row reached out to touch the girl's hand
But she is too lost in the music to know.
He looks at her, and suddenly he is lonely and afraid
Because she has wandered forth into a land
Into which he cannot follow.

The old woman in the black dress shuts her eyes and
remembers.
In her mind, she becomes young and beautiful.
She waits for strong arms to close around her shoulders
And warm fingers to stroke her hair.
She waits.
They do not come.
And she remembers that she is old
And that the arms and warmth and laughter were gone
long ago.
She folds her hands in her lap.

The heavy man with the grimy fingernails slouches in his
chair
And stares past the piano out into the afternoon sunlight.
The crash of factories, shouted orders,
The flash of liquid heat, sweating bodies,
The scream of steel on steel dim in his ears,
And instead he hears wind in trees.

The music swells and rises and fills the room.
Strong hands tear at the piano, coaxing, demanding.
Yielding finally, the hands grow still.

The music hangs suspended, whispers, and grows silent.

The people hang suspended, and then begin to move,
Shoving, laughing, chattering.

The hands at the piano relax.
They belong to a man again.
The man behind the hands comes alive again.
He has a crick in his back.
He wonders what his wife will have cooked for dinner
And hopes it is not fish.

The piano is only a dead black box.

Arnold found the poem pretentious and immediately wrote one of his own. I was incensed. I was supposed to be the writer! He could be musician, philosopher and historian, but I was not going to have him tramping in my territory!

To prove myself, I submitted my poem to *Seventeen*. Arnold sent his to the *Saturday Review*. Both of us got our submissions back by return mail, but along with my rejection slip there was a letter.

"We don't care for the poem," the editor wrote, "but since it is obvious that you have a strong background in classical music, we would like you to write an article on that subject for our April issue."

Now it was Arnold's turn to be furious. Music was *his* terrain!

"You're an imposter!" he accused me. "You'd never even heard of Debussy's music until I took you to that concert! You can't write this article! You'll make a fool of yourself!"

Actually, I had been thinking the same thing. Now, however, my pride was at stake.

"Of course, I can write it," I said peevishly. "All I need is to do a little research."

That "little research" took me weeks. I spent every afternoon and weekend at the library and in record stores. Finally, to Arnold's satisfaction, I had to concede that I was in over my head. He gave me a cram course starting with Schubert's "Unfinished Symphony" and ending with Mozart's "Sonata Number 12." In the end I was able to hammer together a piece that *Seventeen* accepted.

Despite its flaws, I was proud of that article. It was my first published piece of nonfiction—the first story for which I had done research—and my first "assignment." Always before I had written stories first and then gone in search of a publisher. This time, a publisher had *come to me!*

The following summer Arnold's parents moved to another state and put him into private school. For a while we wrote letters, and then we lost track of each other.

Several years ago while researching an article about brain chemistry, I found him quoted as an authority. The magazine credited him with being "Professor of Psychiatry, Neurosciences, Physiology and Pharmacology" and Chairman of the Department of Psychiatry at one of the top medical schools in the country.

For my own part, I'm grateful that I knew him back when he was close enough to my level to enjoy being with me. When I think of classical music, I think of Debussy.

In my novel *Daughters of Eve* there is a scene in which a teenage girl listens to her mother play the piano:

> Holly Underwood sat with her eyes closed, listening to her mother at the piano building Debussy's castle note by silver note to the height of the stars. The room was filled with the ocean, with foam and froth and circling gulls and salt winds whipping icy spray against the palace walls.

When I wrote that scene, it was not a fictional character named Holly who was discovering Debussy. It was a sixteen-year-old girl named Lois, sitting in a crowded auditorium on a Sunday afternoon, learning from a blind pianist that to tell a story it is not always necessary to use words.

7

THE SUMMER OF MY SIXTEENTH YEAR, my parents received an assignment from *Holiday* to do a complete photo coverage of Atlanta, Georgia, and since school was not in session, Bill and I were able to go along. The magazine subleased a house for us. It was in a lovely residential area of the city and served as our home port between photo excursions. It was a fascinating summer that took us from the ghetto to the colonial mansions of the rich.

From my diary, it is evident that I preferred the latter:

> We have been out all day "making contacts" in order to get pictures. Only you just don't *do* things like that in the normal way here! The people are Old South. They live in billion-dollar mansions with great white pillars, all with marvelous histories dating back to before the Civil War, and real bloodstains on the porches made

with real Yankee blood. You don't just introduce yourselves, you have to be formally presented by someone whose grandfather was the friend of someone who was the nephew of the second cousin of a Confederate general. When you finally meet them, the people themselves are warm and sweet and terribly nice.

The first house we saw was at the end of a mile-long lane of blooming magnolias. On one side the lawn sloped down to a lake with swans in it, and there were miles of lovely, twisting garden paths with boxwood hedges that it took over five hundred years to grow, separating beds of flaming canna. On the north there was a whole stable of thoroughbred riding horses and a maze of bridlepaths that entered a woods (all right there on the estate), and when you wandered through the grounds it was like something you dream about—statues—marble fountains—and all of a sudden we practically fell into the largest swimming pool I've ever seen. And it had *tropical fish* swimming in it!

The lady who owned the place must have noticed my expression, because she said, "Oh, my dear, this is only our fishpond! Come, hop into my little runabout, and I'll show you the swimming pool." So we hopped into her "runabout" and were driven a half mile or so to where there were more gardens and a pool that was beyond belief! Mother said, "I bet you spend your entire summer in this!" but the lady said, "Goodness, no! We had it built for our son, but Henry is in Europe now, so nobody uses it."

We all stood there, looking hot and waiting to be invited to go swimming, but that did not seem to occur to her.

Instead, she said, "Do you really mean you want to take pictures *here?*"

Daddy said that indeed he did.

"I can't imagine why!" our hostess exclaimed. "It's nothing spectacular. It's just home, and we live in every corner of it."

How long would it take to live in every corner of such a place!

I wanted to write about that summer in nonfiction form, but I didn't know what direction to take. I wished *Seventeen* would assign the subject, as they had the article on classical music, and give me some instructions about how to handle it, but they didn't even know I was in Atlanta.

One day as I was leafing through a writer's publication, I came across the term "query letter." As I continued reading, I learned that most writers got assignments by writing to magazines and "querying" as to whether or not they would be interested in a particular subject. This letter, the article said, should be a sort of sales letter, in which the writer tried to persuade the editor that his subject was appropriate for the readership of that publication and that he was qualified to write about it.

I immediately wrote three query letters, one to *Senior Prom,* one to *American Girl,* and one to *Seventeen,* with a glowing description of the wonders of Atlanta.

The editors of the first two magazines responded with polite no-thank-yous. The editor of *Seventeen* did too, as far as the idea of a travel article was concerned, but she also said, "What does strike my interest is your mention of spending a morning on Peach Tree Street, tying imported blossoms onto the branches of trees. Is that a typical chore for the daughter of magazine photographers? What other 'behind the scene' anecdotes do you have? If you can come up with sufficient material, I would like to commission you to write a 1,200-word piece about what it is like to be a member of a picture-taking family."

I read the article now so many years later, and I don't like it. There's a cutesy flavor to it, an "aren't we interesting and don't you wish you were one of us" sort of feeling. I didn't mean for it to turn out that way, but I was too inexperienced to know how to avoid it. Even today I find writing that sort of article a problem. The very fact that it's being done in first person makes the writer come across as self-important. If the factual material were stronger and there was a how-to angle it might have gone better, but that, of course, was not what *Seventeen* was after.

Still, as with everything else, I learned through the writing. In this case I learned as well about the use of a query letter to sell work before producing it, and that material for salable articles may be lying right under a writer's nose, overlooked because it is so familiar.

Cameras Are Kings
written at age 16,
published in Seventeen, *March* 1951

"You mean your father and mother are magazine photographers, and you get to travel around with them all over the country? Oh, are you lucky! What a romantic sort of life!"

"Yes," I admit. "It's fun at times."

"At *times!*"

I think back upon the rattlesnakes and Indians, the porpoises and thunderstorms. I remember the hours spent tying blossoms onto peach trees for a "spring" picture taken in midsummer, fanning wilted lettuce leaves to perk up a dying salad for a cookbook illustration, and clinging to a mountain top while Dad snapped pictures of an angry baby eagle.

"Yes," I repeat decidedly, "*at times* it's fun."

And it is.

Magazine photography has a reputation for being a glamorous business in which rich young men click cameras as beautiful models relax in the sun. My parents have taken pictures ever since I can remember, and my thirteen-year-old brother Bill and I have tagged at their heels, carrying camera equipment. I have yet to meet a photographer who was both rich and young, or a model who had time to relax.

We don't travel like normal people. In the back of our station wagon is not only luggage but also nine cameras of assorted sizes, three cases of flashbulbs, three tripods, bags of plate holders, film, electric extension cords, reflectors, and a huge roll of black, backdrop material.

One day Dad came home smiling.

"Guess what?" he exclaimed. "I've bought something that will make our travel much easier."

"A trailer!" we cried excitedly.

No—he had purchased twelve large sponges to place between the cameras so they would not be jolted going over bumpy roads.

We have had many interesting experiences in hotels. One of these was in a little town in Texas where Dad was sent to take pictures of oil wells. No doubt Texas is lovely in the wintertime. The trouble was that we were crossing the Panhandle in midsummer when the temperature was 110° in the shade, and we had all consumed large quantities of greasy Mexican food. The little hotel in which we stayed had one free room which the four of us shared. The furniture consisted of two single beds, a bureau and a spittoon. We were, every one of us, violently ill all night long, but it was impossible to leave the beds because of the camera equipment piled about the room.

Once on an assignment in the Florida Everglades, Bill opened the bag of flashbulbs to replace some used ones. He thrust his hand in and jerked it out again.

"Lois," he said, "there's something alive in there!"

"Don't be silly," I told him.

"There is something in there!" Bill insisted. "There *is!*"

As we watched in horror, a four-foot rattlesnake crawled out of the black depths of the bag and went slithering away.

Another time when we were taking pictures in the Dry Tortugas islands off the southern tip of Florida, a storm came up that opened two seams in the bow of our little fishing boat. We were forty miles from shore.

"What can we do!" Dad cried as water came rushing into the cabin.

"Form a bucket line from the engine room and bail!" shouted the captain. "Bail for all you're worth! When the seas grow calmer, the first mate can swim under the boat and try to calk the seams."

"That's all very fine," Dad responded. "What *I'm* worried about is the cameras! They'll be ruined!"

Few people realize the fakery that goes on in the world of photography. Tying flowers on trees is a minor thing. When you see a picture of a tarpon leaping from the water in a frantic effort to rip the hook from its mouth, how do you think it got there? How did the photographer happen to be focused on that exact spot at that precise moment with the lighting perfect?

On one occasion Dad was assigned such a picture to take. It was Mother who came up with the answer. She went down to the pier and bought a tarpon from one of the fishermen. The following day we hooked the tarpon whom we christened "Hector" to one end of a line and held it out on the end of a jetty. Below the jetty, my parents crouched with their cameras in an outboard, waiting as the cruiser they had hired for the picture drifted into place. When it reached the right spot, Dad would yell, "Throw him!" and Bill and I would heave Hector off the jetty while the cameras clicked. Hector got pretty battered and less appetizing in odor as time went on. It took three days to get the picture Dad wanted. After the first we checked Hector at an icehouse at night.

Posing for pictures is supposed to be glamorous. It isn't. I do it often for the simple reason that pictures sell better if there is a girl in them. On many occasions Dad has said, "I need a figure in that one, leaning on a tree to complete the composition. Get over there and lean!" The thrill passes after you lean on the tree in the blazing sun for an hour. When the picture is published I am generally such a minute part of it that no one recognizes me.

No matter which side of the camera you are on, it's hard work. It's trudging for miles, lugging cameras and film holders, only to find that the beautiful setting you are aiming for lacks the proper splash of sunlight. It's spending long stretches of time crouched in hotel closets, changing film and praying that you won't suffocate. It's adventure—and boredom—stimulation—and exhaustion.

But for all this, Bill and I would never give up the chances we've had not only to live with our parents but to work with them.

8

I REMEMBER THAT SUMMER especially because there was no beach. Every summer before had meant long hours lying in the sand or strolling along the water's edge. In Atlanta the summer was twilight studded with fireflies.

There were maple trees lining the sidewalks. In the evenings after dinner I would go for walks. People would be sitting on porches or washing cars in driveways or mowing lawns, and there was always a crowd of children playing hopscotch in the street. On my way home it would be darker, and the people would be fewer. Lights would go on one by one in the houses. The voices of the mothers of the children would be calling them in, one at a time, until the street would be empty.

In the house across from us there lived a handsome young man who had lost a leg in an auto accident. I never spoke to him as I passed, but I was very conscious of him. He was usually outdoors in the early evening, working on his car or doing yard work.

One time when I walked by, there was a girl with him and they were laughing together.

Of such raw material are stories made.

I wrote the story a year later. The first time I submitted it, it was rejected. I put it away and forgot about it. Years later, I came across it while cleaning out desk drawers, and I submitted it again. This time *Seventeen* not only accepted it, but included it in an anthology of their favorite stories.

I have never understood why they liked it so much better the second time than the first.

Stop Calling Me Baby
written at age 17,
published in Seventeen, *June 1962*

There are eleven maple trees between our house and the Tutters', eleven maple trees and thirty-two cracks in the sidewalk. The summer that I was fifteen the maple trees were green and full and their shade fell in large, dark patches across the hot sidewalk except in the morning when it fell in the street. I must have walked up and down that sidewalk a thousand times that summer, always slowly, always casually, looking at the maples and cracks in the cement.

"Where are you going?" asked Vandy as I pushed back my chair from the table and started to get up.

"Out," I said shortly.

"Where?"

"For a walk."

Mother said, "Karen, you've hardly touched your dinner. Is anything the matter?"

"No," I said irritably. "Nothing's the matter. I just want to go out for a walk. Does anybody have any objections?"

Vandy said, "I'll come with you." She got up too. Vandy was eleven.

"No," I said furiously. "You will not. I'm going by myself."

Vandy's blue eyes filled with tears. She said, "You're horrid. You're always horrid; you never let me do anything anymore."

Mother said, "Karen, don't you think—"

I left the room and went out onto the porch and slammed the screen door behind me. It was early evening. The sun still slanted through the trees and fell halfheartedly on the pavement, the way it does on summer evenings when the dark comes slowly and there is a muffled clatter of silverware and a blur of voices from open doors and windows.

The Tutter house, almost at the end of the block, was larger than ours, although Mr. and Mrs. Tutter lived there by themselves most of the time, with the girls married and Joe away at school. I had never been inside, but I was sure I knew how it would be: a hall and then a living room with a grand piano which Mrs. Tutter sometimes played, and beyond that the dining room. Upstairs the main bedroom looked out over the lawn, and Joe's room was on the first floor around to the side.

Joe was in the driveway washing the car.

I concentrated on the trees as I passed him—ten —eleven—twelve—and I went on slowly to the corner and around it. I stood there quietly a moment. Then I turned and started back.

This time, as I passed, he said, "Hi."

I looked up.

"Hi," I said.

He was bent at a stiff, awkward angle, holding a rag in one hand and the hose in the other, washing the whitewalls. He was wearing an old pair of khaki pants, which covered his legs to the ankles, and a stained white T-shirt. I deliberately kept my eyes from his right leg and focused instead on his bristly crew cut and the nose that was bent a little sideways from football.

"Where are you going?" he asked in a friendly way.

"Nowhere special," I said casually. I crossed over and stood beside him, watching him. "When did you get home?" I asked although, of course, I knew.

"About a week ago. I got a ride down from school with some of the fellows."

"Have a good year?" I asked.

"Sure." He looked up at me and grinned. "What's new around here? Let's see, you must be about in the ninth grade by now, right?"

"Tenth," I said, hating him.

"Tenth? Well, gee!" I hated him more than ever.

He straightened slowly and stood back to inspect

the tire. He gave it a final slosh with the hose. Then he wrung out the rag and went to turn off the water.

"See you around," he said.

I watched him turn off the faucet and walk up the steps—moving stiffly with one hand on the railing—and go into the house. I heard his voice in the living room, saying something and then laughing, and then his mother's laughter. A few minutes later the light went on in his room. I watched the light for a long time and when it finally went off I turned and began to walk hurriedly away. I didn't want him to come outside again and find me still standing there.

It was dusk now. The sun was gone and there were no more shadows, but it was hot. Some little girls were playing hopscotch in the street in front of our house.

Vandy broke away from the group and came over to me.

"Do you want to play?" she asked. She wasn't mad anymore. Vandy never stayed mad.

"No," I said, "I don't."

"You haven't played all summer!"

I started to walk away, and then suddenly I turned back.

"Okay," I said. I tossed in my stone, hopped across the course, turned and hopped back. I picked up my stone and tossed it into the next block. "There," I said, "now I've played. Now leave me alone."

"Okay," Vandy said, "okay. Gosh, you don't have to be so snotty about it."

I went into the house and through the living room and upstairs to my room. Mother and Dad were sitting in the living room, but they didn't say anything as I passed through. I went into my room and closed the door and lay down on the bed. I hadn't eaten much dinner and I was hungry, but I was hungry in another sort of way too. It was a kind of aching feeling, a loneliness that wasn't really loneliness but something else, a feeling of being incomplete. It was a feeling that had started this summer, and it was mixed up in my mind with the heat and the twilight and the maple trees and the children's voices in the street outside.

But it wasn't those things, I thought. Those were a part of every summer I had ever known—they were nothing new. And Joe was nothing new either. He had lived up the block for as long as I could remember. He had washed the car dozens of times and cut the grass and made airplane models in his front yard, and I had hardly noticed. Even that time two years ago when he had been in the automobile wreck—it had been after his senior prom, and I had heard my parents talking about it afterward: "The Tutter boy . . . what a shame . . . to lose a leg at eighteen . . . and I hear he was offered that wonderful football scholarship . . . such a nice, attractive boy . . . such a terrible pity . . ." I had been sorry, of course, but the pain had not been my pain. I was too busy playing hopscotch with Vandy in the street.

I got up and turned on the light and went over to the dressing-table mirror. I looked at myself for a long time. Then slowly I took off my jeans and shirt. I went over to the closet and got the blue taffeta Mother had given me for Christmas and put it on. It was too heavy for summer and a little long; I had never even had it on long enough for Mother to turn it up on me. I went over to my bureau and searched through a top drawer until I found a lipstick.

Vandy came in.

"What are you doing?"

I said, "I thought you were playing hopscotch."

"I was." She came closer. "What are you getting dressed up for?"

"Just because I feel like it. Don't you ever knock before you come into somebody's room?"

Vandy ignored the question. She stood on one foot, as though she were still playing hopscotch.

"They're talking about you downstairs," she said. "Mother and Dad are. Dad says you're acting like a brat this summer and ought to have your bottom whacked even if you are in high school." She smiled importantly. "Mother says to leave you alone. She says you're just going through a stage."

"I'm not!" I said angrily.

"Mother says you are. She says all girls go through it one time or another. *I* won't, though." She looked at me more closely. "Gee," she said, "you look funny in that dress. Your stomach sticks out."

I turned to her in cold fury. "Yours does too," I snapped, and added, "and *you've* got a broken front tooth."

Vandy's hand flew to her mouth.

"I don't," she wailed. "It's only a baby tooth." She was dreadfully self-conscious about her chipped tooth.

"It's not," I said coldly. "It's a permanent tooth,

105

and it's broken, and it can never be fixed, and someday it will die and the dentist will have to pull it, and you'll have a big hole there."

"It won't!" screamed Vandy. "It won't!"

She started to cry and ran out of the room. I watched her go with a stab of guilt. No one in our family ever mentions Vandy's tooth.

I turned back to the mirror. The girl who looked back at me couldn't be called pretty, but she did look different—older—with the bright slash of lipstick across her mouth. I sucked in my stomach as tightly as I could, and the dress didn't look bad at all, really.

"Joe," I said softly, experimentally. "Darling." The sound of my voice saying the words frightened me a little. It was so clear-cut and definite when it was put into words that way. I let myself picture his face, the funny, bristly hair and the clear blue eyes and my throat tightened. "Joe," I whispered again. "I know how hurt you must be—how lonely—how empty life must seem for you, after being a big football hero and everything. You can talk to me—I'll understand. I'll try to—to—comfort you—"

There was a rap on the door.

"Karen?" Mother's voice was brisk. "I want to talk to you."

I didn't answer, and she opened the door anyway and came in. She looked angry. Then she looked at me and saw the dress and the lipstick, and for some reason her eyes softened.

"What do you want to talk about?" I asked coldly.

"You know very well what," said Mother, sitting

down on the end of the bed. "Vandy's in her room crying her heart out because you teased her about her tooth. You know how hard Daddy and I have worked to get her to stop worrying about it."

"Well, that's tough," I said. "Real tough for Vandy. You act as if she's lost a leg or something. If the only thing she ever has to worry about is her tooth, she'll have an easy life."

Mother stared at me as though she hadn't heard me correctly. Then she said, "Baby, what's the matter with you this summer? I don't think I've ever heard you say a thing like that before."

"Nothing's the matter with me," I said rudely, "and, please, stop calling me 'baby.'"

Mother said, "Karen—" and suddenly, unreasonably, my eyes flooded with tears.

"Leave me alone," I said. "Why can't everybody just leave me alone?"

I pushed hurriedly past her and ran downstairs, through the living room and out onto the sidewalk again.

It was night now, but not really dark because of the lights from the houses and the street lights, and the eleven maple trees were huge dark masses against the night. I walked quickly now, not bothering to count them. This time I knew I wasn't going to walk casually past the Tutter house. There was an ache inside me, almost too great to bear, and I knew I had to see Joe. It didn't matter if he thought I was completely crazy. I had to see him or I'd die.

I didn't stop to let myself think about what I was doing. When I reached the house I walked quickly up the porch steps and knocked loudly on the door.

Mrs. Tutter answered it. She came from the living room, calling something laughingly back over her shoulder. She looked out uncertainly through the screen, not recognizing me on the dark porch.

"Yes?"

"I'm Karen Jackson," I said. "From down the street."

"Oh! Well, come in, dear," Mrs. Tutter said pleasantly. "Is it Girl Scout cookie time already?"

I felt my face flush bright red.

"No," I said, "I just—just—" I had an inspiration. "Mother is baking and she's run out of eggs. She asked me to ask you if she could borrow a couple."

"Why, yes, of course," Mrs. Tutter said graciously. "Come in, Karen, and I'll get them for you."

I followed her through the hall into the living room. It was just the way I had imagined it, spacious and pleasant, with a huge piano in the corner. Mr. Tutter was watching television, and there, sprawled on the sofa, was Joe.

"It's the little Jackson girl," Mrs. Tutter said as though she were introducing me for the first time. "Her mother's baking and needs some eggs."

Joe looked up and smiled. "Hi," he said. "I'd hardly have recognized you out of jeans."

"Hi, Joe," I said.

Mr. Tutter nodded at me and turned down the television. "Some of these summer replacements," he said, "are better than the regular programs."

"Yes," I said, "I guess they are."

Joe hauled himself up and motioned for me to sit down at the end of the sofa. The cushion was warm where his good leg had been. He said, "What are you all dressed up for, Karen? Got a heavy date?"

"No," I said. And then I added carefully, "Not tonight."

"Well, you look awfully nice anyway."

"Thank you." I felt happiness rushing through me in a burning wave. It was almost too much to believe that a moment ago I had been moping in my bedroom and now here I sat, in Joe's home, right on the sofa beside him.

I made myself look at him, straight at him. His eyes were as blue as ever, and his crooked nose made him look oddly vulnerable. I longed to take the rough brown head and draw it down to my shoulder and say aloud the words I had practiced in my room.

Someday, I thought. Next summer, perhaps, or the summer after. He is looking at me now and smiling; it is a beginning.

Mrs. Tutter came bustling back into the room. She had a dish in her hand.

"Are two eggs enough, dear? Are you sure that's all your mother wanted?"

"Yes," I said. "Two eggs."

Joe glanced toward the window.

"It's pretty dark outside. Maybe I'd better walk you home."

I thought for an instant my heart was going to stop beating.

"You don't have to do that. It must be hard for

you—I mean, to walk any more than you have to—"

"It'll do him good," Mr. Tutter commented gruffly, his eyes still plastered to the television screen. "He's so restless he's about to tear the house down this summer. Wish Marcy had come home with him as we asked her to."

"She couldn't," Joe said. "You know that. Her mother wanted her to go shopping in New York."

"Don't see why she can't get her trousseau here as well as in New York," Mr. Tutter muttered, but there was a note of teasing in his voice. "The way women carry on, you'd think the poor girl was getting something special, instead of a gimpy, flat-nosed college student with two years to go for his B.A. She must be crazy!"

"She is," Joe said, "about me. Lucky girl didn't even have to run very hard to catch me—I couldn't get away from her."

He grinned and his father chuckled and shook his head. It was evidently a familiar exchange. I stared at them both in bewilderment.

"Marcy?" I said. "Who's Marcy?"

"Joe's fiancée," Mrs. Tutter explained. "No matter what those two jokers say, they don't mean a word of it. Pop's just as crazy about her as Joe is."

"Fiancée?" I repeated the word numbly. "You—you're getting married?"

"This fall." Joe swung his leg off the sofa and got a grip on the arm. He held out one hand. "Want to give me a haul up, Karen?"

I shook my head. "No."

"No?" He looked surprised. "Why—"

"You don't need to walk me home." My voice was ragged and strange to my ears, somebody else's voice. "I like to walk by myself. I like to walk in the dark."

An instant later I was in the hall groping blindly for the door.

"Karen?" Mrs. Tutter's voice flowed after me. "Your eggs!"

The world seemed to be spinning before me. For a moment I clung to the doorknob; then with a tremendous effort I turned and went back into the living room and took the dish with the eggs.

I said, "Thank you."

At home I undressed quickly and got into bed. The sheets were cool. I didn't even bother to turn off the lights; I just lay there feeling the dull ache, the funny, throbbing emptiness. Outside a faint breeze stirred the maples and they rustled, a whispering of leaves moving a little in the summer night, and I thought, "There are eleven maple trees between our house and the Tutters'." Which was a silly thing to think because it didn't matter how far away Joe was, eleven maples or eleven million miles.

I was still lying there with the light on when Mother stopped by the room on her way to bed.

She hesitated in the doorway.

"Karen?" she asked. "Are you awake?"

"Yes," I said.

Mother said, "I thought you might have gone to sleep with the light on." She came over to kiss me good night the way she always did, just as if I were a baby or something. But this time was different. This time I did not mind.

"Mother," I said, "Joe Tutter's engaged. He's getting married."

"Oh, baby," Mother said softly. "I'm so sorry." The way she said it, I knew she understood, that she had understood all along. Suddenly I was crying; deep choking sobs, the way I had not cried for years.

"I love him!" I cried. "I love him so much!"

"I know," Mother said. She did not put her arms around me, she merely sat there and let me cry. "It's hard," she said, "the first time you love somebody. I remember. It's hard."

"It's not the loving that's hard!" I cried angrily. "It's the other part! It's wanting him to love me too!"

Mother was silent a moment. When she spoke again, her voice was very gentle.

"That will come," she said. "In time. They don't always come together, you know—loving and being loved. If they did, there would be no chance for us to grow."

I leaned back against the pillows. Outside the maples moved again, and the breeze slipping through the window was surprisingly cool, almost an autumn-flavored breeze. I drew a long, shaky breath.

"It has been a horrible summer."

"It has," agreed Mother, "for all of us. And the worst of it is, we still have it to live through with Vandy."

She smiled, and suddenly to my amazement I found myself smiling back. We sat there for a long time after that, not mother and daughter the way we had been, but two old friends who had found each other again after a long time apart.

9

I WAS NOT IN LOVE with the one-legged boy in Atlanta. As I've said, I never even met him. But I knew, or thought I knew, what it would be like to be in love with him. I empathized with the girl who was laughing with him in the driveway. Years later the heroines in two of my books would fall in love with physically handicapped boys. In *Five Were Missing* it would be a young man with an arm wasted from polio, and in *Stranger with My Face* it would be a boy who had been badly burned.

"Stop Calling Me Baby" was a title selected by the editors. My own title for this story was "End of Summer." The main thing I knew when I started writing it was that I wanted somehow to recapture the sensations of that Atlanta summer—the slowly deepening twilight—the rustle of the maples—the children's voices ringing out through the dusk. I had never before lived in a neighborhood. Our beach house in Florida was set back from the road, surrounded by sand dunes and sea oats. The idea of so many people living so close together with their lives spilling out through their front doors into the warmth of the summer night was enchanting to me.

I was not happy with the title change. No one had consulted me about it, and "Stop Calling Me Baby" seemed to me to have little to do with the theme of the story. "End of Summer" said it all. When I wrote the editor to ask about this, she replied that she agreed with me, but that "End of Summer" just didn't sound very interesting.

"The purpose of a title," she told me, "is to act as bait, to hook the reader's interest so he will pick up the magazine and start reading. 'Stop Calling Me Baby' sounds as though two people are having a battle and one is shrieking at the other. 'End of Summer' sounds like a pile of dead leaves."

Why were there so few girl friends in the stories from my early years? All the strong relationships seem to be between boys and girls, or between girls and their families. The answer, perhaps, is that I myself had few close girl friends. I ran with a crowd and enjoyed many people in a surface way, but I never seemed to form those deep, all-consuming friendships that most teenage girls make such an important part of their lives. My better friends were those who had strong interests of their own in such things as music, art or theater. And my one real confidante was my mother. Over and over again the heroines of my stories have their problems put into perspective by the wise words of loving and understanding mothers. I didn't have to struggle and deliberate over those scenes. They just seemed natural.

As I shared my life with my mother, she shared hers with me. Here is an excerpt from my diary:

Mother has a jade ring in which there is a tiny miniature of a blond boy's laughing face. The boy's name is John. This is the story:

Mother met John when she took a trip on a banana boat. They fell very much in love and decided to be married. First, however, John wanted to return home and break the news to his parents who planned for him to marry another girl, an old friend of the family. Before they parted, John gave Mother the jade ring and told her, "This is to keep my memory green."

Mother returned to her own home, and she and John corresponded daily. Then Mother went to visit a friend, and John came to spend the weekend nearby. There they completed plans for their wedding. John's plan was to bring his parents to meet Mother, and then together they would break their news. He had already broken up with the other girl.

So Mother and John returned to their

respective homes, and Mother waited for his letter. It did not come. She wrote him and received no answer. After a while she began to realize that she was never going to hear from him—that she had been dropped. Eventually she gave up and married another man whom she learned to love very much. But always there was the pain and wonder about John. She had been so sure he loved her!

Six years later she again met the friend whom she had been visiting when she had last seen John. The friend said, "Wasn't it a shame about John?" "What do you mean?" Mother asked. The friend said, "You mean, you didn't know? It was in the paper. On his way back from his visit with us, the train he was riding went off the track, and everyone in his car was killed."

Mother and Daddy are so happy together, it does not seem possible that there could ever have been anyone else in either of their lives. It is as though they were fated to be together. How strange to think that each might have married someone else!

I tucked away such tales in the corners of my mind as a squirrel does nuts, and in later years I would draw them forth. This particular one was to provide the climax for a story I was to write long after. It would be called "Written in the Stars."

Our Atlanta summer over, we returned to Florida,

where I started my junior year of high school.

Meanwhile, the gentle world I was used to was in the process of changing. The United States had decided that in order to honor its mutual defense treaty with South Korea, it must enter the Korean War.

This was not the first war for my generation. We had been children during World War II, and most of our fathers had served in the military. My own father had been Chief Training Officer at the Naval School of Photography at Pensacola during the year I wrote "The Fairy in the Woods," and the woods I described in the story were on the outskirts of the naval base. But although my classmates and I remembered air-raid drills and food rationing and the glorious excitement of D-Day, for all practical purposes it had been our parents' war, not ours.

The Korean War belonged to us. It was our generation who would be fighting it. To underline this fact, barracks were thrown up at our local airport and an Air Force training program established there. Suddenly our town was filled with young men in uniform, few of them looking much older than high school age. I looked about me at the boys I knew—handsome Don; gentle Roger; Tom, the trumpet player; Fenton, the cartoonist; Bob and Lee and Barry and Sumner—and I tried to imagine them killing people. It was impossible. Still, they were most of them seniors, one short year away from being drafted. And what about my brother? Bill was only an eighth grader, but wars seemed to have a way of hanging on and waiting for people.

The Youth Center was the core of our town's teen social life, and on weekends the servicemen invaded it. Lonely and young and away from homes and families for the first time, they clutched eagerly at the opportunity to establish friendships. The town boys hated them, because they could not compete with the glamour of their uniforms. We girls were overwhelmed by our sudden popularity. Even the homeliest of us had romances followed by long-distance phone calls from subsequent bases and letters postmarked from foreign countries. There was a sense of hysteria about it all, because we knew we operated on a time limit and all our love stories would be left unfinished. We met . . . we touched . . . we parted.

I dated a boy named Dick and one named Ralph and one named Raymond. All eventually ended up overseas, and one did not return. One of my girl friends eloped; the marriage was annulled by her parents. Another attempted suicide when the private she was in love with was transferred to a base in Texas so suddenly that she was not able to say goodbye.

Out of the chaos of my junior year there came a story that won me first place in *Seventeen*'s annual creative-writing contest. It was the first story in many years that I had written from a male viewpoint.

Return
written at age 17,
First Place Winner in Seventeen's *Creative Writing Contest, January 1953*

The curtains were crisp and ruffled at the windows. Outside it was still not quite dark, still just on the edge of twilight when fireflies were beginning to twinkle in the hedge by the walk.

Inside, the kitchen was warm and bright, and the biscuits were baked a little too long, and the woman was smiling across the table while the little boy was feeding a chicken wing to the cat.

Bill looked at them and thought, Well, I'm here.

He thought it in an odd, detached way, as though he were not really there at all.

Last night on the train he had buried his face in the hard Pullman pillow and thought, Just seventeen more hours! Just seventeen more hours and I'll be home! He had seen himself crossing the yard, opening the front door, going into the hall; he had smelled the cedarwood chest and heard the tick of the hall clock. Then he had gone through the living room into the kitchen, and they had all been there —the woman and the little boy and a serious man with graying hair—and they had hugged each other and laughed and eaten supper together in the kitchen with the twilight outside.

Last night he had been terribly excited.

Now he was here, and he was not excited at all.

"What's the matter, dear?" asked his mother anxiously. "Are the biscuits too brown for you?"

"No," Bill said quickly. "Of course not. They're just the way I like them."

"You're not eating very much, dear."

"Yes, I am," said Bill. "You just haven't been noticing."

He helped himself to another biscuit and buttered it industriously.

"Do they feed you biscuits in the army, Billy?" asked the little boy with interest.

"Sure, Jerry, but not like these."

"I remembered how you always liked biscuits," said his mother, "so the first thing I thought when we got your telegram was how we could have biscuits for supper when you got home. Remember how you and your father used to eat two whole plates of biscuits at one meal?"

"Yes," said Bill, and then he said, "It seems odd without Dad."

"Yes," said his mother. "It does."

The light went out of her eyes, but she still smiled, a determined smile.

"I—I didn't get your letter about the accident until six weeks after it happened," Bill went on awkwardly. "We were behind enemy lines and weren't getting any mail. I wrote as soon as I heard."

"Yes, dear, I'm sure you did."

"I guess maybe I didn't sound like I wanted to. I don't write very good letters."

"It was all right, Bill," said his mother. "I understood."

Bill nodded gratefully, but he knew she had not understood, because he had not fully understood himself. There had been a stack of letters at one time, ten from his mother and sixteen from Mary. He had read Mary's first—*Dearest Bill*—chitchat about college, the last football game, Arden and Mike going steady—*I miss you so much. All my love, Mary.* He had read slowly and pictured her as she wrote, her face flushed and pretty, her pen racing along the page as she spilled out her thoughts helter-skelter before they had time to get away. When he had finished, he started his mother's letters—accounts of the Garden Club, Jerry's toothache, a new paint job on the car—and finally, the accident.

The letter about the accident had been heartbreaking and brief.

Bill had read it carefully and laid it aside. He had thought, My father is dead, but he had not felt any great sorrow, only numbed disbelief.

That night he had dreamed about rows and rows of men, all dead, but none of them was like his father. They were young men with drawn yellow faces; and suddenly they weren't dead at all, but twisting and turning and screaming in horrible fits of agony. The dream was so real that he awoke with a scream ringing in his ears.

He had lain very still in his blankets and thought My father is dead. But he could not believe it was true. Death was something close and horrible and frantic, something his gentle, easygoing father could know nothing about.

He had groped for his flashlight and, when he had found it, he had read Mary's letters again. *I miss you so much. All my love, Mary.*

When he had gone to sleep that time, he had not dreamed again.

Bill jumped as the cat wound itself around his leg. "New cat, isn't it?" he asked.

His mother said, "A female cat came along, and Tuffy went away. This is Pepper."

Jerry leaned forward in his seat, a small, pale boy with glasses.

"Billy," he said eagerly, "did you ever kill anybody?"

After a moment Bill said, "Yes."

"With a gun?"

"No," said Bill, "with a bayonet."

His stomach contracted and the chicken tasted like meal.

His mother said, "Jerry, you may excuse yourself and go upstairs to your room. I'll be up to talk to you in a few minutes."

Bill felt the bayonet, warm and strong in his hands. He felt it pressed against him as he ran. He saw a man in front of him, and he watched the end of the bayonet, and he saw the man's face when they met . . .

"Oh, Mother," said Jerry, "why? Why do I have to go up now? It's not even half-past eight yet!"

Bill got up quickly.

"I have to go," he said. "I've got a date."

"But, Bill, you haven't had your dessert yet!"

Bill said, "Save it for me and I'll eat it later. When I talked to Mary on the phone I told her I'd be by at eight-thirty."

He went outside. It was really dark now, and the fireflies were fairy lanterns across the lawn.

Bill stood in the darkness and breathed deeply and the sickness went away. Then he got into the car and drove to Mary's.

Her father came to the door. He was much smaller than Bill remembered him.

"Well," he exclaimed, "look who's here! How are you, Bill?"

Bill said, "It's good to see you."

They shook hands. Mary's mother came in from the kitchen with the two sisters, the one who played the piano and the little one with the braces, only she wasn't little now and the braces were gone.

Mary came in.

She was plumper than Bill remembered, and her hair was cut short and fluffy around her face instead of long over her shoulders, but she was still Mary.

She said, "Hi, there, Bill."

"Hello, Mary."

Then in the car, she was close and warm beside him.

"Where do you want to go?" he asked.

"There's a party over at Anne's. We might go there." She hesitated. "Or we could go to a movie."

Bill said, "Let's skip the party. I'd kind of like to have you to myself this evening."

Mary said, "All right. I think it will be a stupid party anyway, and the movie's a good one."

The movie was terrible. Bill sat stiffly in the cramped seat, conscious of Mary's presence beside him. He could smell her perfume and feel the warmth of her shoulder pressed against his. Finally he stopped all pretense of watching the screen and shifted his full gaze to her and saw that she was crying because the woman in the movie could not make up her mind between the two men.

Bill felt embarrassed. He had forgotten how Mary cried in movies. Before he had always teased her about it and found it strangely touching. Now, suddenly, it was ridiculous.

"Come on, Mary," he said, "let's go."

"This isn't where we came in!"

"We'll see it some other time."

He got up and made his way between the seats to the exit. Mary followed him, pouting.

"Bill, I don't understand what's the matter with you."

"I don't know either," he said apologetically. "I'm sorry. The movie was getting on my nerves, and I wanted to go somewhere quiet where I could just sit and talk to you for a while. I guess I can stand the rest of it, though, if you want to go back in."

Mary sighed.

"No," she said. "Let's do what you want to do tonight."

They got into the car.

He said, "Tonight's the first time I've driven a car for six months."

"What was the last time?"

"It was a Jeep, and I didn't drive it very far."

He drove out along the river road to their old parking place by the water, but when he reached it there were two cars already there. He swore a little under his breath and stepped on the gas.

A side road loomed up on his left. He slowed down, turned the car into it and stopped.

The wind came up from the river and breathed through the car windows, soft and cool.

"Thanks for writing so much," said Bill at last to break the silence.

Mary said, "You hardly wrote at all."

"I know. I didn't have time."

"I didn't either," said Mary. "It's hard to do all the things you really have to do at college, much less write letters. But I *made* time."

"It was swell," said Bill. His voice was strained.

What's the matter with me? he asked himself angrily. I've been away two years, and now I'm with my girl and there's nothing to say!

Always before there had been too much to say, things that would not go into letters when he sat down to write them. He would get as far as *Dear Mary,* and the paper would stare up at him, white and empty, and the things he wanted to tell her would not be written down. Instead he would say, *There have been some men sick,* but never how they looked with the sickness and how they smelled and how he felt when he saw them; or *A man was shot yesterday,* but never a description of a man with half of his face missing, a man who used to chew gum and play a guitar. He did not write, *I'm lonely. I'm sick. I'm scared.* These things he whispered to Mary in the secret night and saved to tell Mary when he got home and they were together.

Now he took a deep breath.

"Mary," he said, "I killed a man."

He waited for her to shiver, to gasp, to be horrified. He waited for the tears that came so easily at a movie.

Instead she said, "I guess everybody did, didn't they?"

"I don't know," said Bill. "I guess they did."

He wanted her to share the horror of it, and in that way perhaps the horror would go away.

"After all," said Mary. "that's what you were there for, to protect our country."

"But he was a man," said Bill, "and I killed him. He was a live man, and now he isn't alive."

He shuddered and the old familiar sickness went through him.

"Bill," said Mary suddenly, "have you met another girl?"

"What?"

"I said, is there another girl?"

For a moment Bill was sure that she was joking, but then he realized that she was not.

"No," he said. "There's no other girl. How on earth could I have met another girl?"

"I don't know," she said. "It's just that you're

acting so odd. I thought maybe you had met some-one else."

"No," said Bill again. "There's nobody but you."

He put his arms around her and pulled her to him and kissed her. When he kissed her the strain went away and the years between them were gone; it was the night of the Senior Prom, and he was very young and in love. He lifted his face and pressed it against her hair, and for a moment he was filled with peace. He was home and everything was all right.

"Mary," he whispered, "oh, honey, I missed you so!"

"I missed you too, Bill."

"Mary," he said, "let's get married. Let's get married now."

He could feel her start.

"Get married?"

"We'd have the rest of this leave together before I have to go back. Please, Mary!"

She pulled away from him and looked at his serious face.

"Bill," she said nervously, "don't be silly. I could-n't stop college and get married now. Daddy would have a fit if I even suggested such a thing. And what good would it do? You'd be away all the time."

Bill released her and leaned back against the seat.

"Yes," he said wearily, "of course, you're right. It would be a nutty thing to do. It's just that you'd belong to me then, and I'd belong to you. Right now I don't feel like I belong anywhere. Everything's so different from when I left."

"I'm not different," said Mary.

"Yes, you are. We used to not even have to talk, we understood each other so well. Now it's like we didn't know each other at all."

"You *do* have another girl," said Mary miserably. "I can tell."

This time Bill did not try to deny it. He started the motor.

"It's getting late," he said. "I'd better take you home."

When they reached the house Mary opened the car door and started across the lawn.

"It's all right," she said. "I can walk to the door by myself."

"Mary!" Bill caught her.

She stopped and turned back to him; there was no anger in her face, only unhappiness.

"Mary, there isn't any girl!"

Mary said, "I know there isn't any other girl. I almost wish there were. At least then we'd know what was wrong!"

Bill stood in the yard and watched the hall light go off and later a light go on upstairs. Then he got back into the car. He started it and pressed the accelerator to the floor and watched the needle creep up across the speedometer. He drove out along the river road again, faster and faster until the sound of the wind past the window was a dull roar. He had driven like this once before, in a Jeep, but suddenly the road had ended and the Jeep had gone off into the underbrush where a man was sleeping. Bill and the man nad stared into each other's faces, and the man had groped in the bush beside him for his gun, and Bill had picked up his bayonet . . .

Bill slowed down and drove quietly back to town. He drove home, because there was no place else to go.

He crossed the yard and went up the porch steps and opened the door. It was like going into a stranger's house, a house that was oddly familiar as from a dream, but not a place where he himself had lived. In his mind were other houses, tumbled masses of houses without walls and without roofs and with all their life gone from them. He stepped into the hall and closed the door behind him, but he could not shut the ghost houses out.

The light was on in the living room. His mother looked up when he came in.

"There's a piece of cake for you in the kitchen."

He hesitated.

"Were you waiting up for me?"

"Yes," said his mother. "I know it's silly, but I couldn't sleep until I knew you were in."

Bill thought, how old she looks! Why, Dad and I always used to think she was the prettiest lady in town!

"It hasn't been easy with Dad gone, has it, Mom?"

It did not sound the way he had meant it to sound.

She said, "No, dear, it hasn't been easy. But we're getting along."

He wanted to go to her and put his arms around

her in a protective gesture, the way his father would have, the way he himself would have so short a time ago. He wanted to say, "Oh, Mother, I'm glad to be back!" He wanted to hug her and say, "Mother, you're still the prettiest lady in town!" But the shadows of the last two years were all about him, close and real and a part of him.

He looked at his mother, and they could not reach each other.

He said, "Mom, have I changed so very much?"

"It's the war, Bill," she said slowly, carefully. "War makes boys grow up too fast. It turns them into men before they are ready and teaches them things they should never know."

"But why?" he demanded unreasonably. "Why? What's the matter with me? What in the name of heaven has happened to me?"

His mother was startled by his outburst.

"Don't look that way, Bill! Everything will be all right, dear. Just give it time and everything will be all right."

He hadn't cried much when he was a child. Now, when he cried, it was the way a man cries when he is lost and afraid.

"Mother," he sobbed. "Oh, Mother, I want to come home!"

She went to him to put her arms around him the way one comforts a child. But he was no longer a child.

"There, there, son," she said helplessly. "You *are* home."

She went out to the kitchen to get his piece of cake.

What was it about this story that caused it to win a major award?

I wish I knew. I have a feeling there was some reason other than the writing. Perhaps it stood out from the others because of the male viewpoint and therefore got an especially careful reading. Perhaps one of the judges had a son in the service. Perhaps the story seemed more important because it was about war and death instead of proms and parties.

Perhaps it was the ending. The ending doesn't follow the rules of plotting that most youth magazines of that day adhered to. For once, I did not have the all-wise mother solve the problem, for the problem is unsolvable. The mother's pathetic token gesture of bringing in a piece of cake is symbolic of the futility of any loving woman's trying to undo the emotional damage done to her son by war. If this story had been submitted by an adult writer, I doubt that *Seventeen* would have bought and published it. They would have thought it too depressing for their vulnerable young readers. The fact that it was one of those vulnerable readers who wrote the story altered the situation.

I named the young man in the story Bill, not because it was my brother's name, but because it was solid, down-to-earth and all-American. The Bill in the story had no personality quirks to set him apart and make him an individual.

He was Every Man.

🌿10

THE TRAINING PROGRAM in Sarasota was only temporary, and after a year the Air Force facilities were moved elsewhere. The town settled back to normal and my classmates and I settled into our senior year emotionally exhausted.

It was a pleasant year, but not a particularly exciting one. I was editor of the yearbook and managing editor of the school paper. A boy named Otto was made editor-in-chief. I was not happy about this, as I had always assumed that when I was a senior that position would be mine.

"The editor-in-chief is always a boy," the journalism teacher explained patiently. "Managing editor is a more active position anyway. You'll get to lay out the pages."

I liked laying out pages, but I would have liked even better issuing assignments. Otto was bright and intellectual, but his achievements in the field of writing were minimal, and I could see no reason why the simple fact that he was male should make him more fit for editorship than I was.

The journalism teacher would not be reasoned with.

"That's just the way it is," he told me.

So I became managing editor and enjoyed it, although I never did get over my feeling of resentment when I saw Otto standing there with his assignment sheet, handing out orders to his reporters.

With the Air Force boys no longer available to date us, and last year's seniors now graduated and gone, my girl friends and I faced a year of comparative old maid-hood. Most of the boys our age were dating girls from the younger grades, and the pickings were slim. What with all the natural pressures of senior year and the approaching college entrance exams, this didn't bother us too terribly until springtime when the Senior Prom appeared on the horizon. Then suddenly we became frantic. It was imperative that we attend the prom! It was a landmark occasion! It was the party to end all parties, held in our honor, and to miss it was worse than death!

The teachers tried to help us as best they could by barring sophomores from the dance, thereby forcing those boys who were dating beneath their age group to escort a senior. There were also a few senior boys who, for one reason or another, never dated at all. These were the misfits or the late bloomers, shy, short or unsociable. Up until now we had hardly looked at them. Overnight, they became prizes to be won at any cost. We curled our hair, glopped on mascara, and descended upon them. It was one mad scramble.

I cased the situation quickly, selected my prey, and leapt. He never knew what hit him.

His name was Sumner, and he was one of the shy ones. He was also the younger brother of one of the teachers. He was quiet and sweet and had beautiful brown eyes and extremely long lashes. I was the first girl he had ever dated.

On our tenth date he asked if he could kiss me good night.

"My sister says it's time now," he told me solemnly. Then he stood there, waiting for instructions.

The kiss was awkward, but rather lovely, and from then on we were "going together." I taught him to dance, and we went to the prom and to the breakfast afterward. We walked together at graduation, swam and sailed together during the summer, and parted with fond goodbyes to attend different colleges. There was not enough substance to the relationship to carry it over into the next chapter of our lives.

Before I left for Duke University, I wrote a story called "The Last Night." It was an autobiography and a prediction, all in one. It was also a thank you to my family and, in a way, a goodbye.

The Last Night
written at 18,
published in Seventeen, *September 1953*

Anne is asleep. She sleeps quietly, lying on her side with one hand under her pillow. Her hair is rolled tight in pincurls. Tomorrow it will lie soft and curly over her shoulders, but tomorrow night I shall not see her, for she will be gone. I watch her sleeping tonight as I have done so many years before, warm and close and all around her; for I am a part of her, and she is a part of me.

I am Anne's room. I am light blue walls and blue curtains and a bureau on which sit a comb and brush, a pink stuffed elephant, a picture of Larry and a container of bobby pins. I am a bookshelf which is two shades of blue, because Kendal started painting it and never got around to finishing. I contain a battered copy of *Robin Hood,* several volumes of poetry by Edna St. Vincent Millay, *Gone with the Wind,* a stack of paperback novels, and a rhyming dictionary. I am a rug with a nail polish stain on it, a scarred old desk full of letters and diaries and scrapbooks, the folding alarm clock Anne's father gave her when she was graduated from high school, and the silver inkwell which she never uses but won in an essay contest.

I have changed since yesterday, for clothes have been taken from my closet and packed in the two suitcases which lie open in the middle of my floor, and a new dress of a kind Anne has never owned before hangs on the closet door. Anne will wear it tomorrow.

But for tonight she is still mine, and I watch her as she stirs and smiles in her sleep. I know what she is dreaming, for I have known her for a very long time. . . .

Anne enters for the first time. She is a fat little girl with braces on her teeth and tight brown braids, and she bounces when she walks. She wrinkles her nose because I am not as large as she wanted me to be.

"The walls must be blue," she says at once. "I want the walls painted blue."

"Mother won't let you," says Kendal, who stands in the doorway with his hands in his pockets. "She says we're going to leave the walls just the way they are."

"No," declares Anne. "They will be blue."

"Mother!" screams Kendal in his high, shrill, little-boy's voice. "Anne says her room's got to be blue!"

Their mother's voice comes wearily, answering from downstairs where she is hanging curtains in the dining room. "We'll have blue curtains and a rug, and some of the furniture will be blue."

"No," says Anne firmly. "The whole room. Everything in the whole room must be blue."

She walks over to my window and looks out into the yard.

"There's a swing!"

"Is there? Where?" Kendal flies to the window too, and pushes in beside her. "Oh, I see. You can't ride that, Annie! You're too fat!"

Anne gives him a slap and Kendal screams, "Mother!" But when there is no answer, he says, "Let's go play."

Their footsteps clatter on the stairs, and a moment later I hear their voices out by the swing. Kendal is saying, "You see! I told you! You're too fat!"

I have another occupant now. He is a dog named Turvey. Turvey is supposed to be half Kendal's dog, but he much prefers Anne who feeds him and brushes him and lets him sleep at the foot of her bed. Anne is going to be a veterinarian when she grows up and run a boarding kennel for dogs.

Kendal comes in often and sits on the bottom of Anne's bed and swings his feet while she tells him stories. The stories are always the same—full of dragons and giants and princes on horseback—but even so, Kendal often gets so excited that he bounces on the bed until the springs creak. Turvey always leaves when Kendal comes in.

I see their mother once or twice a day when she comes in to bring clean laundry and to hang up Anne's pajamas and straighten her bed. She thinks Anne is old enough to do these things herself. Anne means to, but she usually forgets.

I scarcely ever see Anne's father, because he works in a law office all day and comes home just in time for dinner, after which he sits in the living room with Anne's mother for a while and then goes to bed. Occasionally he will rap sharply on my door at night and say, "Daughter, it's time your light was off." Then Anne will say, "Yes, Daddy," and turn off her light for a few minutes and when he is safely gone she will turn it on again.

Turvey is not quite housebroken yet, but he is still only a puppy.

Anne is getting ready for a dance. She is putting on lipstick in front of the mirror. Her hair is not in pigtails now; it is combed back from her face and held with a ribbon, and her dress is soft and fluffy and blue and swishes when she moves.

She steps back from the mirror and looks at herself.

"Mother!" she calls. "Mother! Come look! I'm beautiful!"

Her mother comes in, and her face goes warm and soft.

"Darling!" she says. "You will have a wonderful time!"

"Of course," agrees Anne.

They go downstairs together and I hear Anne's father start the car in the driveway.

Her mothers says, "Be careful of your dress when you shut the door."

The car leaves, and I wait.

Turvey comes in and jumps onto the bed. He lies on the pillow because he knows no one will come in and tell him to get down. There is a little pool of pink nail polish on the rug where Anne spilled it in the excitement of getting ready.

Time passes. The clock in the downstairs hall

strikes eight and nine and ten and eleven. The lights go out in the house next door.

I hear the car in the driveway again. The door opens and closes.

Anne's father says, "You're sure I didn't come to get you too early? The other kids didn't seem ready to leave yet."

"No," says Anne.

Anne's mother calls from her room. "How was it, dear?"

"Fine, Mother."

"Come in and tell me about it."

"Some other time," says Anne. "I'm very sleepy."

Her mother's voice is disappointed. "All right, darling," she says. "Goodnight."

Anne opens my door, and she is not beautiful anymore. She is only a plump little girl in a tight blue formal with too much lipstick on her mouth.

Turvey, looking guilty, gets off the pillow quickly and moves to the foot of the bed. Anne throws herself down beside him and buries her face against his back and begins to cry.

"Oh, Turvey," she sobs, "I'm *fat!*"

All at once, Turvey is dead. He was run over by a milk truck early this morning, and Anne's father found him in the road on his way to work.

Anne does not own a black dress, but she ties a black ribbon in her hair.

Kendal is crying very loudly.

"He was half mine," he sobs.

"No," says Anne. "He was not yours at all. He was all mine because he loved me the best."

"He didn't!" wails Kendal. "He didn't! He didn't!"

Suddenly Anne goes to him and puts her arm around him.

"No," she says quietly, "of course, he didn't. He was *our* dog and he loved us both the same."

They bury Turvey in the yard out behind the swing.

This summer I do not see much of Anne. She blows in and out, very tall and tan in her white tennis shorts and bright-colored halters. Her braces are gone now and she wears only a retainer at night after she goes to bed. Although her mother has taken in all her clothes, they still seem to be baggy around the waist.

When I do see her she is usually with another girl and they are talking and giggling. Someone named Jed has given Anne a pink stuffed elephant, and Anne and the other girl laugh a lot at that.

"Oh, what a romantic thing to give a girl! An elephant!"

"What on earth did you say when he gave it to you?"

"Say? Why, I said, 'Oh, Jed, every time I look at it it will remind me of you.' "

"Anne, you didn't!"

"Of course, I didn't, silly. I said, 'How cute.' What else could I say?"

The telephone rings a lot.

"Anne, it's for you!"

"Who is it?"

"I don't know!" shouts Kendal into the receiver. "It could be any of them. You've got so many, I can't keep them straight!"

Kendal, too, has changed. He is taller than Anne now and his treble has dropped to an uncertain rumble that breaks occasionally into a surprised squeak.

He waits while Anne talks. Suddenly his grin fades and he looks worried.

"Annie," he says when she hangs up, "you don't ever let those guys kiss you, do you?"

Anne looks surprised.

"Some of them," she says. "Once in a while."

"Which ones?"

"Only Peter and Jed. And only sometimes."

"Well, I don't think it's right," says Kendal in a fatherly tone. "I don't think you should let any boy kiss you until you're really in love with him."

Their father comes in on the end of this.

"Hello," he says. "What's the conversation about?"

"Nothing," says Anne.

"Nothing," says Kendal.

They smile at each other, and their father is awkward and out of it all, very much apart. He shrugs his shoulders, turns away, picks up the evening paper.

Anne is writing an essay. She writes slowly, breathing hard, leaning forward over her desk.

At first she writes with difficulty, but then suddenly the words begin to come. They begin to fall into a pattern, to say what she wants them to say. Her pen races across the page and the lovely words pour onto the paper swiftly, easily, beautifully; and she writes faster and faster in a glow of wonder.

Kendal comes to the door.

"Dinner, Annie."

"Go away."

"Aren't you hungry?"

"No."

He leaves and a few minutes later her mother appears.

"Is anything wrong, Anne? Are you sick?"

"No, I'm busy."

Her mother says firmly, "Come to dinner this minute before everything gets cold."

Anne sits at the dinner table without speaking, eating nothing, trying to keep the spell from breaking.

Her father says, "What's the matter, daughter?"

"Nothing."

"She's writing something," says her mother.

"An essay," says Anne. "For a school contest."

"How nice."

They finish dinner and Anne comes again to her desk and reaches for the words. They are still there, shining and golden at her mind's edge. They tremble on her pen and dance onto the paper. She finishes one page and lays it aside and begins another and finishes that and begins another. Her pen runs out of ink. She fills it again and writes on.

At last she is done. She picks up the papers and goes into the hall.

"Mother!" she calls, but to her amazement the house is dark and silent. She looks at the hall clock and it is a quarter to three.

She goes to her parents' door.

"Mother," she calls softly, "I've finished the essay!"

"Fine, dear. I hope you win." Her mother's voice is thick with sleep.

"Mother, it's good. It's very good. I can tell." Her voice is leaping with excitement. "Mother, I know what I am going to do! I'm going to become a writer!"

But her mother is fast asleep.

She comes to me again and lays the pages on the desk.

"Goodness," she says, "I'm hungry!" She smiles happily.

It is a hot day. The gown is long and white and woolen. Anne hates wearing it because the heat makes it itch, but there is nothing she can do about it.

"At least, let me wear the cap back on my head," she says snappishly as her mother pushes it forward.

"Anne, it's not *supposed* to go on the back. It's supposed to sit perfectly flat on top."

"But then I don't have any hair sticking out at all. I look like an egg."

Kendal comes in. He grins.

"Well, look at that! The sweet girl graduate in person!"

Her father comes to the door. He stands there for a long moment, not saying anything. He is looking for a child, but there is no child to see. There is a tall, young woman in a cap and gown who smiles at him as though she knows him very well; but he does not remember ever having seen her before.

He says, "Daughter, I have something for you, a little present." He holds out the alarm clock. It is little and silver and lovely in its leather case. The case is blue.

Anne cries, "Daddy! Oh, Daddy!"

She runs to him, and he knows her again now. Her mother and Kendal gather to examine the present. They are all close together, warm and laughing, the four of them; and their laughter flows through me until I am warm and very full.

I am waiting. I am still Anne's room. I am still full of Anne's things, but Anne is absent. She writes often from college, but her letters are usually read in other parts of the house, and all I know of them is from scattered remarks I hear as people pass by my doorway.

"I'm glad she likes her roommate." "I hope she won't start smoking." "Larry Chockworth. Odd name—Chockworth. She says he's very nice. But then she used to say that Jed was nice too." "How much did she say that sorority would cost?"

I am waiting. I am still Anne's room, but I am not complete until Anne is here.

Anne comes home for Christmas vacation. She is glad to be home, and she hugs her family and hangs tinsel on the tree and goes skating with Kendal and his girl and she teases her father and laughs with her mother; but she is different. She is no longer all theirs. Her mind is full of things they do not even suspect.

"Mother," Anne says, "I am not so sure now about being a writer."

"Why, darling? I thought you had definitely decided."

"I don't know now. So many people are better than I am. Sometimes I think it would be better to let other people write the books and just be one of the people who reads them."

"Well, it's up to you, dear."

After a moment Anne says, "I think you would like Larry. The boy I wrote you about."

Then she laughs and begins to talk about other things. She talks about so many things that when she leaves her family is not quite sure which were the important ones or if any of them were important at all.

Kendal is painting the bookshelf as a surprise for Anne when she comes home for spring vacation. He has it only half done, because the paint is too thick and he has to keep thinning it with turpentine.

His mother comes in.

"Kenny," she says quietly, "you won't have to hurry with that shelf. I just got a letter from Anne, and she won't be home for spring vacation. She's been invited to spend the two weeks at Larry's home in North Carolina."

Kendal dangles the wet paint brush in one hand.

"You're not going to *let* her!"

"Yes," says his mother. "If that's how she wants to spend her vacation, I want her to do it."

"But she ought to come home. She can see him all year long at college."

His mother sighs and he puts his arm around her awkwardly.

"Gee whiz, Mother," he says. "I'm still here."

His voice is deep now like his father's, and his shoulders are broad, and his long face crinkles up when he smiles.

His mother says, "Oh, Kenny, I'm so glad I have a daughter *and* a son!"

Anne has come home again, but she is not alone. She has brought a boy with her. He is a slender, quiet boy with blue eyes and a shy smile. Her father likes him. Kendal likes him too, despite himself, for he was all set to dislike him intensely. Anne's mother is not sure whether she likes him or not.

I see very little of Anne now. She comes in late at night and undresses slowly and goes to bed. Her body is slender and strong and lovely, but she does not know this yet. Sometimes she stands in front of the mirror and says, "Oh, dear, I am too thin!" in just the way she used to croon, "I am too fat!"

"Oh," she whispers, "I want so to be beautiful!"

It is the last night before they return to college. It is not really night at all, but early morning. Anne comes in softly and closes the door. Her face is soft with wonder and her eyes are shining. She stands alone in the middle of my floor and looks at the ring

The diamond burns and glows and fills me with its splendor, although it is only a tiny diamond.

"Oh," whispers Anne. Her joy is bursting within her, too great to bear.

"Oh," she whispers, "I love you! I love you!" and her voice leaps and sings, and she is half crying and half laughing at herself for being silly enough to cry, and she is too happy to care.

I draw about her and hold her close, because I know that soon she will be mine no longer. Soon she will be gone. . . .

Anne is asleep. She stirs and smiles, for she is dreaming.

She has forgotten a broken swing and a dog named Turvey and a fat little girl in her first dance dress. But she will remember them again; for they are part of her, just as she is part of me.

I wait. Before long the sky glows red and the room begins to grow light. A milk truck rumbles down the street outside. A dog barks to be let out. Somewhere a baby cries.

Sunlight steals in the window. It rambles idly across the half-filled suitcases on the floor and beams on the creamy satin wedding dress where it hangs on the closet door. Then it climbs to the bed and tumbles carelessly across Anne's face.

She stretches and yawns and opens her eyes.

"Oh," she says joyfully, "what a lovely day!"

A story written in this style would never appear in a magazine today. Even in children's publications it's no longer acceptable to have inanimate objects thinking and speaking as though they were human. I wrote it this way because I needed a frame, something to encase the fragmental scenes of my story and hold them together.

I was also feeling sentimental. I *liked* the idea of my room's missing me when I was gone.

🌿11

MY PARENTS HAD ALWAYS TAKEN IT FOR GRANTED that both Bill and I would go to college. Daddy had graduated from Princeton, and Mother had attended Smith and been one of the first class of exchange students to graduate in Paris. Education was a tradition in our family, and I moved automatically from high school into the college of my choice, just as I had moved from grammar school into junior high.

It was a total surprise to discover that I was out of place there.

It wasn't the classes themselves that created the problem. Those I found interesting, especially the English and history. What I missed was my own space. At home I had had my own room and a tremendous amount of privacy. At Duke, I shared a room with a girl named Muriel, and a suite with girls named Lydia and Barbara, and a bathroom with thirty other girls on our hall, in a dormitory that vibrated day and night with the endless chatter of female voices.

All of our time was scheduled. Not only were there classes, there were dorm meetings, campus meetings, and religious services. There was constant togetherness. Girls flowed in and out of each other's rooms as though they were common territory, and each person's phone calls and callers were announced over a loudspeaker, so even those were in a manner shared. We ate together, studied together, exercised together, and brushed our teeth standing in a row in front of a line of basins. If you were noncommunicative, two dozen well-meaning dorm mates asked anxiously what the matter was. If you closed yourself in your room for twenty minutes, people rapped on the door to find out if you were "all right in there."

Within weeks I was longing desperately for the ocean—the long stretch of empty beach, the whisper of waves and the cry of gulls—and solitude.

To make things worse, all the girls I met looked alike to me. Back in high school my visual memory problem had not affected my life too greatly because I'd been with the same classmates from seventh grade through twelfth. Since the school was a small one, they had become as familiar to me as members of my family. At Duke I felt I was drowning in a sea of faces that ran together into a churning, gibbering blur. Rush week was traumatic. I couldn't tell one set of sorority girls from another. I tried to peg them by heir clothing—"The one in blue is Marcia; the one n green is Valerie"—but since they never wore the same outfits twice, this was useful for one party only. The callbacks were the worst. Because we had been ntroduced previously, it was assumed that we now knew each other. I faked my way along as best I could, trying to avoid situations in which I might have to refer to someone by name. We were supposed to circulate, but I was terrified to do so for fear the person I approached might turn out to be the one I had just finished talking with.

Several times this did happen.

"Hi! I'm Lois Steinmetz from Sarasota, Florida!"

"I know. You just told me."

The whole thing was a nightmare. It was like playing a word game in which everyone but you has had a look at the answer sheet.

When bids came out, I did receive one, but I declined it. It seemed hypocritical to pledge my undying loyalty to a sisterhood whose members I couldn't recognize when I met them on campus.

And I couldn't write! That was the most frustrating thing. Oh, I cranked out term papers at appropriate intervals, but I didn't consider that real writing. It wasn't communication, because no one got to read them except the graduate assistants who graded them. It seemed a waste to me to spend days dredging up information and setting it on paper if nobody was going to publish it. Originality was frowned on. I wrote a term paper for Shakespeare class on Othello and Desdemona, using the "Can This Marriage Be Saved?" format from *Ladies Home Journal*. The professor was horrified. For Milton I wrote a fifteen-page rejection letter from the *Saturday Evening Post*, detailing the reasons the story wouldn't make it in today's market:

> You have a problem with word repetition. Do you realize there are 127 references to the word 'light'? I gather from the fact that the manuscript was typed in Braille that you have personal reasons for this preoccupation, but the imagery needs to be varied or it loses its effectiveness. Some careful cutting is advised. . . .

I thought it was funny, but nobody else did.

My own writing was impossible for me. My mind was numb, and my ears were ringing. In order to be creative, I needed time alone, and that was one thing college life did not provide. Neither did it provide freedom. I had thought somehow that leaving home would be a giant step toward independence, but found myself under stricter chaperonage than my easygoing parents had ever provided. Each time I left the dorm I had to sign out, giving my destination and expected time of return, and when I came back I had to sign back in again. There was a ten o'clock curfew on weeknights and a one o'clock on weekends. Male callers were permitted no farther than the parlor, and the whole lawn in front of the dorm was covered with floodlights so that goodnight kisses could be carefully monitored.

When I went home at Christmas, I told my parents that I thought one year of college might turn out to be all I wanted.

They regarded me blankly.

"But, if you drop out, what will you do?"

It was a question I could not answer. What *could* I do except move back home again? I knew I wanted to write, but I was beginning to wonder if that ability had deserted me, as I had written nothing for months that was of publishable quality. I had never held a job. How could I support myself? I had some confused idea that it might be nice to go to New York and become an editor, but I did not know how to go about it. And if I did go, where would I live? This was an era in which eighteen-year-old girls did not have their own apartments. They lived at home until they were married. Much as I loved my family, I had no desire to go back to being a child in their home. I wanted to be an adult in the adult world, and that world was not Duke University.

I returned to college, made the honor roll with my first semester grades, and started dating a senior pre-law student. Buzz was attractive, intelligent and charming. He was also very persuasive—and I was at a point in life when I was vulnerable to persuasion. When he proposed, I said, "Yes." We were married in May, three weeks before his graduation and four days after my nineteenth birthday. My parents were not happy, but they accepted the inevitable and gave us a beautiful wedding in the Duke Chapel. Muriel was my maid of honor. Lydia and Barbara and the other girls in the dorm gave me a shower. My high school friends sent cards and presents and congratulatory notes that were tinged with envy. Roger sent a gold bud vase and a letter saying that he would love me forever but wanted me to be happy.

Was I in love? I certainly thought so. On looking back, it seems strange that I should have followed the story line of "The Last Night" so exactly without having subconsciously planned it that way. It was as though I had written my own script and was now setting out to play the role I have given myself. And I had cast Buzz as "Larry."

I had begun to write again: not stories, but odes to the Prince Charming who would be to me what my father was to my mother—lover, friend, companion, confidant—and would bring me, as all fairy-tale princes brought their princesses, happiness ever after.

Discovery
written at age 19

I, who was never beautiful before you came;
I, who turned my face when loveliness passed by,
Oh, suddenly, there is nothing in the world more
beautiful than I!

This body which has lain asleep so long—
Now it is waking and stirring and searching for the
            light.
In all the years that passed, I never knew
My legs were long and slim, my arms were white,
That I had breasts and velvet skin and lips that
            could be stirred to flame.

I, who was not beautiful before you came,
I stand before the window by my bed
And feel the evening wind against my hair,
And now my body is a wondrous thing, too marvelous
            to bear,
And I must run and dance and laugh and cry
And tremble at this beauty which is I!

I am a silent bird who finds that it can sing.
I am a tree who stood all winter long with branches
            cold and bare,
And now I wake—and it is spring!

Buzz was a member of the R.O.T.C. unit at Duke, so when he graduated he automatically became a second lieutenant in the Air Force. He went through a short training program in Georgia, during which time I stayed with my family, and he then was sent to upper New York State. I accompanied him there, and we lived in a boardinghouse in a room that was decorated with the huge head of a stuffed elk. It hung there opposite our bed, staring down at us with glazed glass eyes. I was allowed use of the community kitchen for fifteen minutes each evening, and since I didn't know many fifteen-minute recipes, we ate out a lot.

Buzz was athletic—something I hadn't counted on. He had down-pedaled this trait while we were dating, but now it rose to become a regular part of our lives. Fun, for Buzz, was hiking. And mountain climbing. And hunting. He hunted with a bow, and assumed that I, naturally, would do so too. And I did. I carried my own bow and marched along beside him through the forest, looking for things to kill. I never managed to hit anything, but I did learn to pull the arrow back far enough so that it didn't fall directly to the ground. And when Buzz killed a rabbit, I skinned it. And cooked it. And threw up at the table.

From New York, Buzz was transferred to Livermore, California. There we rented a two-room apartment, a guesthouse stuck out behind a private residence, and I became a housewife. My day began at six in the morning when I got up and fixed breakfast. Then Buzz took the car and left for work and I cleaned up the apartment. Cleaning two rooms does not take long. It was done by seven-thirty. Which left nine and a half hours to fill—with nothing.

With *nothing?* Why wasn't I *writing?* I, who had despaired of college because the pressures were so intense that I could not be creative—now I had all the time in the world, and I couldn't write a word. It was as though, suddenly, there was nothing feeding *in*. The days were long and empty. There was no one to talk to, not even a dorm mother. Buzz had to take the car, so there was no place I could go. If I'd had the car, I don't know if I would have used it—where *would* I go, in this strange place where I had no friends? I was not secure enough to know how you went about going forth and meeting people when there was no one to start you off. I attended the officers' wives group at the base when they had their monthly luncheons, but they all looked alike, and my old childhood shyness was back upon me. I didn't know what to talk about. Most of the wives were older than I, with growing families. They had been everywhere and seen and done everything. They played bridge (I didn't), and played tennis (I didn't), and when, occasionally, some kind soul would see me sitting in my corner and ask me what I "did" and I said "write," it seemed to finish off the conversation.

On one occasion, a woman took it that one step further.

"What do you write?" she asked.

"Magazine stories," I said.

She gave me a long, disbelieving stare and transferred her attention to the other end of the table.

I missed my family. And I missed my ocean. The poems from that period are mostly about the beach.

A Child, Moving Inland
written at age 19

We lived by the sea for so many years
That she stopped noticing long ago
The swish of water against the rocks
And cries of gulls when the tide was low.

She never heard, when she lay in bed,
The seawind whispering past our door
Or constant murmuring all night long
Of restless waves on a sandy shore.

It's only since we have come away
That we find her listening for the sea.
I think she never had guessed before
How strangely silent a night can be.

We did not stay long in Livermore. Buzz was transferred to a base in Everett, Washington, where we rented a small house. Now there was more housework with which to fill the empty hours, but for a Home Economics flunker, cleaning was not too fulfilling. I suggested looking for a job, but Buzz preferred that I didn't, since he worked erratic hours and liked me to be at home when he was. Besides, he reminded me, there was little chance anyone would hire me since I had no training in anything and had dropped out of college. I wrote a couple of short articles, one for *Compact* offering advice to college freshmen, and one for *Seventeen* called "Before You Marry."

"All girls, everywhere, have one thing in common. They dream of being married someday," is how that piece began. I then went on to advise all young women to spend their teen years learning to be homemakers.

"A man who wants to enter a profession realizes that he must devote time to learning it thoroughly before he can ever hope to be a success," I counseled sagely. "The same is true of a girl and her marriage. Being a wife is one of the most important jobs in the world, and to be a successful wife a girl must go through a period of training. When the right man arrives on the scene, you want to be ready."

Although I sold the articles, I took no pride in them. They were dreadful, and I knew it. I couldn't understand it. Why wasn't I writing well? Why wasn't I happier? I was holding the pot of gold at the end of the rainbow. I had a handsome husband, a cute little house to fuss around in, all the trappings that went with the role of an adult woman. Why did I feel so empty and dissatisfied?

Something was missing, but what was it?

I settled upon the same answer as millions of other young women.

I had a baby.

12

ROBIN WAS UNDOUBTEDLY THE MOST BEAUTIFUL BABY in the world. I wasn't the only one who thought so—my mother did also. She flew out to be with us during the first hectic weeks, and together we hung over the crib, exclaiming over the tiny, heart-shaped face, the huge brown eyes, and the full head of glossy dark hair.

"I made her!" I told myself ecstatically. *"I made this person!"*

Suddenly the days were filled with activity. There were bottles to sterilize and formula to mix; there were the bath and the feedings to administer, the diapers to wash and fold; there was the daily airing when I wheeled my miracle child in her carriage relishing the admiring comments from passersby.

And I was writing again! Strangely enough, now that my free time was limited, I was writing richly and happily. When Robin went down for her naps, I flew to the typewriter and worked steadily until she woke up.

Buzz was the proud father during the early weeks, but became less enthusiastic when the realities of parenthood came home to him. No longer were there quiet, candlelight dinners. Evening was Robin's time to exercise her lungs. No longer was I free to go hiking and hunting and target shooting at a moment's notice, nor could we go casually to a movie or dancing at the Officers' Club. Robin was not a healthy baby. She was born with a kidney problem, and I spent many nights walking the floor with her and bathing her to bring down fevers. It is not particularly romantic to sleep with a woman who is constantly jumping out of bed to see to a howling infant, and Buzz became increasingly more resentful.

One evening when he came home from work and I suggested he go in and see the baby, freshly bathed and dressed, waiting in her crib, he regarded me coldly.

"I saw the kid yesterday," he said. "Has she changed any since then?"

I laughed as though he were joking. He *had* to be joking, didn't he? All Daddies adored their children!

Soon after that, I wrote a story called "Written in the Stars." I drew upon several past experiences, fragments of things: my first dates with Sumner, a story my mother had told me, an experience one of my friends had had when she and her high school boyfriend attended different colleges.

That was all the story was supposed to be.

When I read it now, however, many years later, I find something in it that I do not think I meant to put there.

Written in the Stars
written at age 20,
published in Seventeen, *November 1959*

Ever since I was very little, I knew that someday my prince would come. At first I used to envision him riding up on a snow-white horse to scoop me up and carry me away to his castle. This changed, of course, as I grew older and my reading matter progressed from *Grimm's Fairy Tales* to *Romeo and Juliet.* I did away with the horse by the time I was eleven, but the rest of the belief remained, a quiet certainty deep inside of me. Somewhere in the world there was The One, the special One, looking for me just as I was looking for him, and someday he would come. It was written in the stars.

I never talked about it much, except once in a while to Mother. I dated just as the other girls did, strings of silly, uninteresting little boys, just to kill time until The One arrived. And then, when I was seventeen, two things happened. Mother gave me the locket, and I realized who The One was. Ted Bennington.

When I opened the little white package on my seventeenth birthday and saw the locket, I was flabbergasted. The locket was not a new purchase; I had seen it often before. In fact, every time I rummaged through Mother's jewelry box to borrow a pair of earrings or a bracelet or something, I saw it, not in the jumble of everyday jewelry but in the separate little tray where she kept all the things Daddy had given her. There was the whole story of a romance in that tray—Daddy's track medals from college and his fraternity pin, the pearls he gave Mother on their wedding day and the silver pin from their fifteenth anniversary and the silver bars he wore when he was in the Navy during the war. And in the midst of all these things was the locket.

"But, Mother," I protested, holding it up in amazement, "you can't really mean for me to have this! It's yours! It belongs to you."

"Indeed, I do," Mother said decidedly. "It represents a lot to me, honey. I've always said that my daughter would have it when she was seventeen." There was a faraway look in her eyes.

"But why seventeen?" I asked. "That's hardly a milestone like sweet sixteen or eighteen or twenty-one. Seventeen really isn't anything."

"It was to me," said Mother. "It was the age of heartbreak."

I stared at her in disbelief. "Your heart was never broken!"

It was impossible to imagine Daddy, with his warm gray eyes and gentle smile, ever breaking anyone's heart, least of all Mother's. Mother and Daddy had one of the best marriages I have ever known. They always seemed to have fun together, no matter where they were or what they were doing. And they loved each other. You could tell it just by being around them. It wasn't the grabbing, hanging onto

165

love of kids our age, but it went deeper; it was the sort of love that made Mother say two years ago when Daddy died, "Well, I've had more happiness in my eighteen years of marriage than most women have in fifty."

"Oh, it was broken, all right," Mother said lightly. "And yours will be too, dear. It's inevitable." Then she kissed me.

I laughed, a little embarrassed, because we're not usually a very demonstrative family. Besides, I wasn't quite sure what Mother was talking about. But I did love the locket. It was tiny and heart shaped on a thin gold chain, and it was delicate and old-fashioned and lovely. I felt about it the way Mother did about her engagement ring—"much too valuable just to wear around." I wrapped it in tissue paper and put it in the corner of my top bureau drawer.

The locket wasn't the only present I received on my seventeenth birthday. Besides that, Mother gave me an evening dress, ankle length, dark rose taffeta and Nancy, my best friend, gave me the rose slipper to wear with it. But the gift that topped everything, that caused my stomach to lurch and my heart to beat faster, was a simple blue scarf with a gold border. It came from Ted Bennington.

"I hope you like it," he said awkwardly. "I didn't know. I haven't had much experience picking things out for girls."

"I love it," I said warmly. "It's just beautiful."

I suppressed a desire to lean over and kiss him. It would have been so easy to do because I liked him so

166

much. I liked the way his blond, curly hair fell forward over his forehead, and his honest blue eyes and nice, square chin. And I liked his being shy and sweet and serious and a little awkward; it was so different from the smooth know-it-alls in our senior class. I thought, I *would* like to kiss you, Ted Bennington. But I didn't say it. And I didn't kiss him.

Instead I reached over and squeezed his hand and smiled at him and said, "It's beautiful" again. Which must have been the right thing to do, because he squeezed my hand and smiled back at me.

I had begun dating Ted a couple of months before that. It was funny how it started. Ted must have been in my class for years and years, and I never really noticed him. In fact, nobody noticed him. He was a quiet boy and he wasn't on any of the teams or in the student government or in any of the clubs; he worked after school and on weekends in Parks Drug Store. I think that might have been one of the things that made him shy, having to work when the other kids goofed around. "It made me feel funny," he told me later, "having to serve Cokes and malts and things to the kids and then seeing them in school the next day. You can't actually be buddies with people who leave you ten-cent tips."

"But none of the other kids felt like that," I told him. "They never gave it a moment's thought. They would have been glad to be friends anytime if you'd acted like you wanted to."

"I know that now," Ted said. "But it took you to show me."

Which was true. It was cold-blooded in a way. I

didn't have a date to the Homecoming Dance, and I was on the lookout for someone to take me. You don't have too much choice when you're a senior and most of the senior boys are going steady with juniors and sophomores. So I made a mental list of the boys who were left and crossed off the ones who were too short, and that left four. Ronny Brice weighs three hundred pounds and Steven Porter can't stand me and Stanley Pierce spits when he talks. Which left Ted.

"Do you know if Ted Bennington's asked anyone to the Homecoming?" I asked Nancy.

Nancy gave me a surprised look. "Who?"

"Ted Bennington," I said. "The blond boy in our English class. The quiet one."

"Oh," Nancy said. "I didn't know that was his name. No, I don't suppose he has. He doesn't date, does he? I've never seen him at any of the dances."

"No," I said slowly, "I suppose he doesn't. But there's always a first time."

The next morning I got to English class early and as Ted came in I gave him a real once-over. I was surprised. There was nothing wrong with his looks. He wasn't awfully tall, but he had a nice build and good features and an honest, clean-cut look about him. I even liked the back of his neck.

Ted Bennington, I thought, you may not know it now, but you are going to take me to the Homecoming Dance.

And I managed it. It is a little shameful to me now to think about how schemingly I managed it—a smile here, a sideways look there, "Hi, Ted," every time I passed him in the hall, "What page did she say we were to do tonight, Ted?" as we left class and happened to reach the door together. A week or two of that and then the big step. "Nancy's having a party this weekend, Ted. A girl-ask-boy affair. Would you like to go?" It was really pretty easy.

Ted was standing at his locker when I asked him. He had the door open and was fishing out his gym shorts, and when he turned he looked surprised, as though he were sure he had not heard me correctly.

"Go? You mean, with you?"

"Yes."

"Why—why, sure. Thanks. I'd like to." He looked terribly pleased and a little embarrassed, and I wondered suddenly if he had ever taken a girl anywhere in his entire life.

"What night is the party?" he asked now. "And what time? And where do you live?"

We stood there a few minutes, exchanging the routine information, and I began to wonder if maybe I was making a mistake asking Ted to the party, to that particular party anyway, because it would be The Crowd, the school leaders, the group I had run around with since babyhood. And Ted wasn't one of them.

But it was too late then, of course, to uninvite him, so I let it go, trying not to worry too much as the week ended, and on Saturday night at eight sharp Ted arrived at my house.

He made a good impression on Mother. I could see that right away. He had that quiet air of formal politeness that parents like. When we left, Mother said, "Have fun, kids," and didn't ask, "What time will the party be over?" which is how I could always tell whether she really liked my dates.

Ted didn't have a car, so we walked to Nancy's, and it was a nice walk. Everything went off well at the party too. The Crowd seemed surprised to see Ted at first, but they accepted him more easily than I had thought possible. Ted relaxed after the first few minutes and really made an effort to fit in; he danced and took part in the games and talked to people.

Even Nancy was surprised.

"You know," she said when we were out in the kitchen together getting the Cokes out of the refrigerator, "that Ted Bennington—he's really a very nice guy. How come we've overlooked him before this?"

I said, "I don't know." I was wondering the same thing.

I wondered it even more as we walked home afterward, talking about the party and school and what we were going to do after we graduated, comfortable talk as if we'd known each other forever. I told Ted I was going to secretarial school, and he told me he was working toward a scholarship to Tulane where he wanted to study medicine. I learned that his mother was a widow, as mine was, and that he had three sisters, and that he played the guitar. The moonlight slanted down through the branches of the maples that lined the street, making splotches of light and shadow along the sidewalk, the air was crisp with autumn, and I was very conscious of my hand, small and empty, swinging along beside me. His hand was swinging too, and after a while they sort of bumped into each other. We walked the rest of the way without saying much, just holding hands and walking through the patches of moonlight.

The next morning Nancy phoned to ask if Ted had invited me to the Homecoming.

"The Homecoming? Why, no," I said, "he didn't." And to my amazement I realized that I had completely forgotten about the Homecoming—that, now, somehow, it didn't matter very much.

When the time came, of course, we did go, but now that I think back on it, I don't think Ted ever did actually ask me. We just went, quite naturally, because by then we went everywhere together.

When did I realize that he was The One? I'm trying to remember. I guess there was no special time that the realization came. It just grew, a quiet knowledge deep inside me. It grew out of our walks together, long hikes through the autumn woods with the trees blowing wild and red and gold against the deep blue of the sky, and winter picnics with The Crowd, sitting on blankets around a fire with snow piled behind us and Ted's arm around my shoulders. He brought his guitar sometimes to those, and we all sang.

"Why didn't you tell us you played the guitar?" somebody asked him, and Ted grinned sheepishly and said, "I didn't know anybody would be interested."

It grew, the realization, through the long lovely

spring days and easy talk and laughter and a feeling of companionship I had never known before with any boy, or for that matter with any girl, even Nancy. One Sunday evening (we had been to church together that morning, and to the beach all afternoon and to an early movie after dinner) Ted said, "We fit so well together, you and I," and I said, "Yes," and he said, "It's as if it were meant to be that way."

"You mean," I said, and the words came haltingly to my tongue because I had never said them aloud to him before and I was afraid they would sound silly, "You mean, as though it were written in the stars?"

Ted was silent a moment and then he said, "Yes, I guess that's what I mean."

It was the night of the Senior Prom that Ted saw the locket. As I said before, I didn't wear it often, it was too valuable, but somehow the night of the Senior Prom seemed right. I wore my rose evening dress and my rose slippers and no jewelry except the locket on its slender gold chain.

Ted noticed it right away.

"Nice," he commented. "Makes you look sort of sweet and old-fashioned. Is it a family heirloom?"

"More or less," I said. "Daddy gave it to Mother, and Mother gave it to me." I touched it fondly.

Ted was interested. "Does it open?"

"I don't know," I said.

"Let's see." He reached over and took the locket in his hands, the gentle, capable hands I had grown to know so well, and fiddled with it a moment, and it fell open on his palm, disclosing a tiny lock of hair.

"So," he said, smiling. "I didn't know your father had red hair."

"I guess he must have when he was young. He got gray very early." I smiled too. "Put it back, Ted. It belongs there."

He did so, closing the locket gently as though anything that had meaning for me had meaning for him also.

I'd tell you about the summer, but it is too hard to describe. I think you must already know what it's like to be in love. You get up in the morning and shower and dress and eat breakfast just as you always have before, but every motion, every ordinary thing, is flavored with excitement. "I'm going to see him today—in two hours—one hour—ten minutes—and now he is here!"—a warm, glow inside you, a silent singing. That was the summer—and then, so terribly soon, it was autumn again.

Ted got his scholarship. His face, when he told me, was shining with excitement.

"How do you like the sound of it—*Doctor* Bennington!"

"Wonderful," I said. "Marvelous! But I'll miss you."

"I'll miss you too." He sobered. "I'll be home on vacations."

"Sure," I said. The summer loomed golden and glorious behind us; there would be other summers.

"I wish—" His voice trembled slightly. "I wish you were going to Tulane too."

"I'll be here," I said, "to come back to. I'll be a

secretary in a year, you know. Maybe I can come and get a job with some connection with the college."

"That would be great." Still he did not smile. "I'm afraid," he said suddenly.

"Afraid of what?"

"Of going. Of leaving you here. I'm afraid something will happen, you'll meet somebody else or something. What we've got, you and I—it's so right —so darned perfect! We can't lose it!"

"We won't," I said confidently. You don't lose something that is written in the stars.

And so my prince rode away on his snow-white horse, and that was the beginning of the end. We did not marry. If we had, I wouldn't bother telling this story. Ted went to college and I to secretarial school, and we wrote letters at first constantly, and then not quite so often. Ted couldn't afford to come home at Thanksgiving, and when he did come at Christmas I had the measles (horrible thing to have when you're practically grown), and we did not really get to see each other until spring vacation. By then we had been so long apart that we spent the whole vacation getting reacquainted, and then it was time for Ted to go back again. He was as good and sweet and wonderful as ever, you understand; we just felt as though we didn't know each other quite so well.

"Don't forget me," he said a little desperately as he left.

And I said, "Of course not," but this time I did not sound so sure.

As it worked out, it was Ted who met somebody

else; he who had been so worried, and I had been so sure! But in the end it was he who wrote the letter. The girl, he said, was a premed student just as he was. Her name—well, I've forgotten her name—but she was small, he said, and had hazel eyes and was smart and fun and easy to talk to. I would like her, he said. We were a lot alike in many ways. He said he was sorry.

It was raining the day the letter came. I read it in the living room and then gave it to Mother to read and went upstairs to my room.

I lay on the bed and listened to the sound of the rain and thought how strange it was, how unbelievable. I didn't hate Ted; you don't hate somebody as wonderful as Ted. I didn't even hate the girl. I was too numb to feel anything; I didn't even cry. I just lay there listening to the rain and thinking, he was The One—we were right—we fitted—we were perfect. Now he is gone and he was The One, and he will never come again.

I was still lying there when Mother came in. She did not knock, she just opened the door and came in and stood by the bed looking down at me. Before she said it, I knew what she was going to say.

"There will be other boys," she said. "You may not believe it now, but there will be."

"Yes," I replied. "I suppose so." There was no use arguing about something like that. "Ted was The One," I said. "There will be other boys, sure, but he was The One."

Mother was silent a moment. Then she said, "Do you still have the locket?"

"The locket?" I was surprised at the question. "Yes, of course. It's in my top drawer."

Mother went to the bureau and opened the drawer. She took out the locket and brought it over to the bed.

"Put it on," she said.

"Now?" I was more surprised. "But, why? Why now?"

"Because," Mother said quietly, "this is why I gave it to you." She put the locket in my hands and sat down on the edge of the bed, watching me as I raised it and put the chain around my neck and fumbled the tiny clasp into place. "You see," she said when I had finished, "that locket was given to *me* by The One on the evening of our engagement. We couldn't afford a ring right then. The locket had been in his family for a very long time."

"Oh." I reached up and touched the locket, feeling a new reverence for it. I thought of Daddy drawing it from his pocket, nervous, excited, watching Mother's face as he did so, hoping desperately that she would like it. Mother and Daddy—young and newly in love, two people I had never known and would never know.

"He was everything," Mother continued, "that I ever wanted in a husband. He was good and strong and honest, he was tender, he was fun to be with, and he loved me with all his heart. He was without doubt written for me in the stars." She paused and then added slowly, "He was killed in a train wreck three weeks after."

"He *what!*" I stared at her in bewilderment. "But you said—I thought—" I realized suddenly what she was telling me. "You mean it wasn't Daddy? You loved somebody before Daddy, somebody you thought was The One, and then—"

"I didn't just think it," Mother interrupted. "If I had married him I'm sure I would have been a happy woman and loved him all my life. As it worked out, three years later I married your father, and I have been a happy woman and loved *him* all my life. What I am trying to tell you, honey—" She leaned forward, trying to find the right words— "There is no One. There are men and there are women. There are many wonderful men who can give you love and happiness. Ted was probably one of them, but Ted just came too soon."

"But," I protested weakly, "that's so cold-blooded, so sort of—of—" I felt suddenly as though I were losing the prince on the snow-white horse, the dream that was bright with the wonder of childhood.

"I'm saying," Mother said gently, "that there are many men worthy of loving. And the one of these who comes along at the *right time—he* is the one written for you in the stars."

She went out then and closed the door and left me alone, listening to the rain and fingering the locket. I stared at the door that Mother had just closed behind her.

And then I began thinking of the other door, the one she had just opened.

* * *

Was I beginning to question, without allowing myself to realize it, the rightness of that step I had taken so hastily and so blithely? If I had waited until I was wiser, more mature, better educated, might I have chosen differently?

Was this young man with whom it was beginning to seem I had so little in common, really The One who was written for me in the stars?

13

AFTER BUZZ'S STINT IN THE SERVICE, we returned to Florida where he entered law school and I gave birth to another little girl. She had blue eyes and a pixie face framed in blond curls, and I named her Kerry.

It was wonderful being back on my own home ground. Though we were in a different town from my parents, we were close enough for frequent visiting, and the beach was near. My grandmother had died while we were in Washington and had left both Bill and me a small inheritance. I used mine to make a down payment on a house directly across the street from the law school. Buzz went to classes, played tennis, and partied with his fellow students, most of whom were single. I wrote and took care of babies. During one of our visits to my parents, I discovered that Mother had kept all the letters I had written her during my year at Duke. When I read them over, it was like reading about someone else. Some of the things the girl who had written the letters told about I had completely forgotten. Using the letters as a basis, I began to outline a book about a girl from Florida who went to Duke University and fell in love with a senior pre-law student. I named the girl "Joyce" and gave her a roommate named "Stella" who was much like Muriel. I had no real belief that the book would ever be completed, but I enjoyed working on it when the children were napping.

Aside from my writing projects, I was totally wrapped up in my daughters. There were several other young mothers living in our neighborhood, and we would discuss colic and toilet training while our husbands talked torts and tax law. I didn't realize how shallow we must have sounded until I overheard Buzz one day commenting to a friend that "It's nice for women to have babies, because it gives them something to talk about."

The words were a shock to me. Was I really all that boring? Was it because I was a woman, with women's interests, or because I was *me?*

I began to have nightmares about my decision to drop out of college. There was one version that occurred over and over. In it, I was back at Duke, and it was exam time, and when I looked at the schedule I discovered that I had finals in three different classes that I hadn't remembered I was enrolled in. I had never attended. I didn't even know what the subjects were. I would awake in a cold sweat with my heart pounding, because I was flunking, flunking, flunking, and there was nothing I could do about it.

It was at this time that I wrote a story called "Home to Mother." I think I wrote it to convince myself that my housewife existence was meaningful. Since the story was not about teenagers, I could not submit it to my usual markets, and I sent it, instead, to *McCalls*.

I expected it to be rejected, and I was stunned when, instead of the familiar brown return envelope, I received a telegram:

VERY MUCH LIKE YOUR STORY HOME TO MOTHER FOR MCCALLS. IS $850 AGREEABLE AS TO PRICE? PLEASE ADVISE.

Eight hundred and fifty dollars! It was hard to imagine so much money existed! We were living on the three hundred a month Buzz received from the GI Bill, plus the small amount I was earning selling juveniles.

I wired back:

YES. $850 IS ACCEPTABLE.

That night, at least, I didn't have my nightmare.

Home to Mother
written at age 22,
published in McCalls, *May 1957*

She could not bear it. She knew it the moment she

opened her eyes and saw the glare of sunlight on the walls of the new apartment. Not only were the walls yellow, they were a dirty yellow, decorated with occasional lighter squares showing where previous tenants had hung pictures and mirrors. In contrast the cherry curtains, which had looked so charming in the other apartment, made sickening splotches of color at the windows.

Lee took one long look and shut her eyes again.

"I can't face it," she whispered. "I just can't face it again this morning."

But even as she spoke she was fumbling for her slippers, for Lynda, who had not yet adjusted to the time change between the coasts, was wailing for her breakfast.

Rick was still asleep, a pillow over his face. Lee resisted a nasty impulse to bang something loudly enough to wake him. Instead she plucked Lynda from her current bed, a blanket wadded between two chairs, and carried her out to the living room to change her diaper. She paused en route to stick a bottle into a pan of water on the stove. The stove was part of the so-called "kitchenette"—a rather fancy name, Lee thought, for a living room wall turned into a kitchen. The burner did not work, and she cursed it under her breath and moved the pan to another burner.

By the time she had changed Lynda's diaper, plus her nightie and undershirt, which were also soaking, the water had reached a boil. She took the bottle out of it, and Rick appeared in the doorway just in time to see her pour the water into the coffeepot.

"That's the same water you had the bottle in," he said accusingly.

"So?"

"So, I don't care to have Lynda's bottle in my coffee water."

Lee said, "The bottle's perfectly clean. And even if it weren't clean, the boiling water would kill any germs. There's nothing for you to get so picky about."

"I don't want her bottle in my coffee," Rick said again, turning back into the bedroom. "Did you press my uniform?"

"No," Lee said. "How on earth could I press your uniform when we didn't bring the iron with us? Remember, I wanted to bring it in the car, but you said to let the Air Force ship it."

"The car was so darn full of stuff anyway, especially with that folding baby carriage your mother sprang on us at the last minute." Rick scowled at himself in the mirror. "I can't wear this wrinkled thing. It's still got creases from the suitcase."

Lee said, "There's not much you can do except wear it, unless you want to go to work in your underwear."

She gave Lynda her bottle and changed her again and propped her up on the sofa. She got some eggs out of the refrigerator and put two pieces of bread in the oven to toast. Rick came out of the bedroom, dressed in the wrinkled uniform, and sat down by the card table.

"Did you put fresh water in the coffee?" he asked.

Lee said, "No. There's nothing wrong with the water that's in there."

"I don't want any coffee then, thanks," said Rick. He pushed the cup away and reached for a piece of toast.

Lee sat glaring at him in cold fury, trying to think of something to say that would make him as angry as he had just made her. She found it.

"This apartment," she said, "is the most gruesome thing I have ever seen. And the neighborhood is just plain slummy. Two stove burners don't work and the walls are hideous, and I just can't stand it."

"Well, you'll have to stand it," Rick said coldly. "Apartments around Air Force bases are expensive, and this is the best we can afford."

"We could afford something nice," she said bitterly, "if you'd let Mother help out a little the way she offered."

"Well, I won't," said Rick. He shoveled in a few mouthfuls of egg, finished his toast and got up. "I've got to go," he said, "or I'll be late."

Lee watched as he carefully put on his jacket and the silly little blue cap. As he turned to kiss her, she said, "What about Lynda, Rick? Is it fair to the baby to live in a place like this?"

He straightened up again abruptly.

"You know," he said, "the main reason I was so keen on your coming with me was because it meant that for once—the first time since we've been married—you'd be out from under your mother's thumb. I thought maybe, if you had a chance, you'd grow up and stop being a temperamental bride and start being a wife. Well, I can see I was wrong. You won't change. I don't know if you can't or if you don't want to."

He turned without kissing her and walked out. It was very dramatic, like something from the movies. The only thing that spoiled the effect was Lynda, who had been lying contentedly on the sofa the whole time. Now when the door slammed, she began to scream.

Lee went over and picked her up.

"Okay," she said. "Okay. Quiet now, baby. Everything's okay."

If I were home now, she thought miserably, I'd call Mother. She'd know what to do.

She could almost imagine herself doing it, in the cozy East Orange apartment with the soft tan rugs and the spotless, cream-colored walls. The telephone had been on a little stand in the corner right beside the rose armchair. She would settle herself comfortably in the chair and dial the familiar number, and her mother's voice would answer, warm and comforting.

"Hello, baby. How's everything this morning?"

And Lee would say, "Rick and I just had another jim-dandy of a fight. What do I do now?" She would say it laughingly, because nothing was ever really terrible when she could talk to her mother about it.

"Well, goodness," her mother would say, "you're starting pretty early in the morning, aren't you? What's it all about?"

And Lee would tell her, and somehow with the

telling it would become trivial and even amusing. They would talk about it a little, and then Lee would say, "Lynda's yelling her head off," and Mother would say, "Maybe her formula's too strong. Why don't you try cutting down on the syrup?" Or she would tell her about the apartment and her mother would laugh and say, "Sounds ghastly. Why don't I come over this afternoon and we'll see what can be done about it? Sounds like new curtains and furniture and a new paint job would do wonders. My treat, of course. It'll be fun."

"But I can't phone," Lee said aloud, pushing the daydream abruptly from her. "We don't have a phone, and if we did, we don't have the money." She had no idea what a call between California and New Jersey would come to, but she could imagine. And she could imagine Rick's face if she spent the grocery money on a phone call.

She went over to the refrigerator and got out the remains of a jar of strained pears and sat down beside the screaming Lynda.

"Here," she said. "Breakfast." She supported the baby with one hand and spooned the pears into her mouth with the other. Lynda choked, sputtered, and began to swallow. By the time the pears were gone, she was asleep.

"Thank goodness," Lee breathed. She eased the baby back down on the sofa and glanced hopelessly around the apartment. There was so much to be done, yet so little that one could actually do.

If we were home, she thought, I would vacuum,

but of course the vacuum hasn't been shipped yet. I suppose I could unpack the suitcases.

They had been living in the apartment for two days but she still had not unpacked the two large suitcases—only the small one that had necessities in it. She walked to the bedroom door and looked in. It was a dark little room, and the suitcases stood awkwardly in the small space between the bureau and the bed. She stood regarding them a moment and then abruptly turned and began to make the bed.

"If I unpack them," she said out loud, "and then we move, I'll just have to pack them all over again." Unpacking was a finality. Once their clothes were actually hung in the tiny closet, they were settled; it was a final admission that this was where they were going to stay.

When she had finished in the bedroom, Lee moved on to the living room and emptied Rick's eggs into a paper bag and put it in the corner to be carried out to the garbage can. She poured the coffee into the sink and washed the coffeepot, along with the two plates and plastic forks. She put Lynda's bottles into a pan of water and set them on the stove to sterilize.

While she was on the subject of Lynda she hesitated by the sofa and counted the dwindling supply of diapers. There were four.

"That's just a couple of hours' worth," said Lee worriedly. "I'll have to get hold of a diaper service, and soon."

There was a pay phone booth outside the filling station three blocks down the street. She and Rick had used it to call about having the electricity turned on. But three blocks was a long way when it meant leaving Lynda in the apartment alone. And holding a baby in a phone booth and trying to put coins in and dial was not easy.

I'll try the landlady, Lee thought. She's sure to have a phone.

She glanced at the sleeping Lynda and then slipped outside, shutting the door quietly behind her. The sun, which earlier had shone for an hour, had disappeared, leaving the sky overcast and the air cold and damp.

Lee shivered as she descended the steep stairs and crossed the yard to the main house.

"Where," she asked herself miserably, "is the beautiful California weather they're always talking about? New Jersey may be cold in winter, but it's not as wet and nasty as this."

The landlady answered her knock too quickly.

She must have been sitting at the window, Lee thought, watching me come down, the snoopy old thing.

Aloud she said, "Mrs. Dorrin, may I use your phone?"

The woman stared at her. "Who are you going to call?"

Lee swallowed the impulse to say, "None of your darned business," and tried to smile politely. "I want to get hold of a diaper service. Our baby has just about run through her supply."

Mrs. Dorrin shook her head.

"You won't find one," she said. "Livermore's a real small town, miss. Here people does their own diapers."

"Oh." Lee hesitated. "Is there—I don't suppose there's an automatic laundry close by, is there?"

"No."

"You mean I'll have to do them by hand?" She could not keep the horror from her voice. Lynda gaily soaked through at least fifteen diapers a day.

"Well," Mrs. Dorrin said slowly, "I suppose I could let you use my washer. It's not an automatic now, and you'll have to pay for the hot water and bring your own soap with you."

Lee felt relief sweep over her.

"Thank you," she said. "Oh, thanks."

Mrs. Dorrin was still staring at her.

"You're mighty young, aren't you," she said, "to be married and have a baby and everything?"

Lee flushed with anger, but at almost the same instant she heard another voice, her mother's, saying almost the same thing. Of course, then it had been, "I'm eighteen!" and her mother had said, "But you seem younger, Lee. You're still a baby in so many ways. You're not ready to be married yet."

That was the first time she had ever opposed her mother. Usually she did not have to; they were so close and thought alike in so many ways. But now suddenly there had been another voice to consider —Rick's.

"Sure, you're eighteen," he had said. "You're not a little girl anymore. You're a grown woman. You're plenty old enough to have your own husband and your own home and your own life."

And because she loved Rick she had held out with a stubbornness that had surprised all three of them. Her mother had argued and pleaded and finally given in, and Lee had her own home and her own husband. Rick had found a job with an insurance company in East Orange, marking time until he was drafted, and Lee and her mother had found an apartment. An adorable one.

"You just can't not like it!" Lee had exclaimed in disbelief. "Why, it's perfect!"

"Of course, I like it," Rick explained patiently. "It's swell. The only thing is, honey, we just can't afford it. Not on what I'm making."

"But Mother wants to help us," Lee said. "She says it's important for young people to start life together living in a nice place. She says the first year is something you always look back on, and you want it to be as wonderful as possible."

"Well, sure," said Rick, "but it can be wonderful no matter where we live. You're married to me now, honey, remember? Wherever we both are, that's home. You've got to live on what I can afford."

The argument was settled a week later with the discovery that Lee was pregnant. She was not just pregnant; she was miserably pregnant. Her "morning sickness" was not confined to mornings; it went on morning, noon and night, and she lost ten pounds during the first month.

Of course, Rick gave in about the apartment then.

"Sure," he said. "Whatever you say. You're having

a tough enough time without having to give up this place. I guess your mother is right, in a way. It's swell of her to help out, and we might as well accept it and live really well now. I'll be drafted soon, and then you'll have time enough to learn what it means to be an enlisted man's wife."

To everyone's relief the morning sickness disappeared after a couple of months, and Lee found herself enjoying the rest of her pregnancy immensely. It gave her a thrill of pride to walk down the street and meet her old high school teachers, the policeman on the corner, her mother's bridge-club friends, all the people who had known her so many years. Now there was a new note in their voices when they greeted her. Instead of, "Hi, Lee. How's school?" it was, "How are you, Lee? When is your baby due?"

"I never felt so important before in my whole life," she told Rick laughingly one evening. "I'll almost be sorry when the baby's born and I get back to normal again."

Rick gave her an odd look. "You don't really mean that!"

"No," Lee said quickly, "of course not. I was just joking."

But she could not help gloating at the look of stunned respect in the eyes of her former classmates as they returned from college for spring vacation, and she wore like badges of honor the pretty smocks and maternity skirts her mother had made for her.

One morning two days before the baby was scheduled to arrive, Lee developed cramps.

"It's probably just indigestion," she told her mother on the phone, "but I thought I'd better check with you anyway. I'm here all alone."

"What is it like?" her mother asked cautiously. "Little aches, fairly low down, maybe every half hour?"

"No," Lee said, giving a sudden gasp. A moment later she continued, "Pretty bad aches, low in my stomach, every three or four minutes."

Her mother made a strangling noise.

"Lee, don't you move. Just sit there and don't move. I'll be right over."

It was six blocks from the house to the apartment, and her mother made it in a little over three minutes. Despite the fact that she had not stopped to comb her hair, put on lipstick or button the top two buttons of her dress, she came into the apartment with such an air of calm efficiency that Lee, who had suddenly been swept by a wave of panic, gave a sigh of relief.

"I'm glad you're here," she exclaimed, catching her mother's hand. "Mother, is it going to be bad?"

"It will be the biggest, most exciting thing that ever happened to you," her mother said quietly. She put her arm around Lee. "Can you walk down to the car, darling, or shall I carry you?"

She was twenty-five years older than Lee, two inches shorter and at the moment ten pounds lighter, but Lee never doubted for an instant that, if it were necessary, her mother was quite capable of lifting and carrying her all the way downstairs and out to the car.

However, she said, "I can walk, if we just wait a minute."

They waited until the next contraction was over and then started for the door. Halfway across the room, Lee stopped.

"Rick!" she exclaimed. "He'll want to go over with us. I'll call him."

Her mother gave her a gentle shove toward the door.

"Honey, if you don't want to have this baby in the car, you get going this minute. I'll phone Rick from the hospital as soon as we get there."

"But my bag! It's not even packed!"

"I'll come back and pack it for you," her mother said. "You won't need it for a little while anyway. Now come on."

They reached the hospital at ten-twenty. Lynda was born two minutes before noon.

"It's a girl," Lee said, slightly disappointed. "A little one, too—only six pounds."

"Darling." Rick was bending over her, his face white and strained. "I came the very second your mother called me. I—oh, Lee, honey, was it bad?"

He looked younger than Lee had ever seen him. She reached for his hand, trying to think what to say. She wanted to tell him, to share it with him, this miracle of the baby's birth. She wanted somehow to draw him into it with her and make him a part of it. But when she spoke, only her mother's words came to her lips.

"It was the biggest, most exciting thing that ever happened," she said softly. "I'll never forget it, Rick."

His eyes filled with pain.

"And you had to go through it alone, the beginning part when you were scared and didn't know what to do."

"I wasn't alone," Lee corrected him, "after Mother got there. She took care of everything. All I did was sit there and contract."

"But *I* wasn't there!" Rick exclaimed in an agony of self-reproach. "I shouldn't have gone to work this morning. You said you felt funny when you first woke up, but I never thought—I mean, it was two days early and the doctor said the baby would probably be late—"

"I know," Lee said soothingly. "I never thought it was—this either. But Mother got there so quickly I hardly had time to think."

"But why," Rick asked, "did you call your mother instead of me? You did have the office phone number. I could have been home in ten minutes."

"I don't know. I—I guess it was sort of automatic. I—I mean—" Lee was confused. It seemed so silly to try to explain it. Of course she had called her mother. Her mother always knew how to handle things. She had not even bothered to think about it; she had just dialed the familiar number that meant "home."

"She had been through it herself," she finished lamely. "I mean—well, you wouldn't have known if it was really labor any more than I did."

"No," Rick agreed slowly, "I guess I wouldn't have."

Things were surprisingly easy when Lee came

home from the hospital. Lynda was a good baby and slept straight through the night from the time she was two weeks old, and in the mornings Lee's mother would come over and help with the formula and the housework until Lee was back on her feet. After that she was in the apartment less often, but she had Lee and Rick over to dinner twice a week, happily baby-sat with Lynda anytime and was always on call when emergencies such as colic, diarrhea or diaper rash arose.

Lynda was three months old when Rick's draft notice arrived.

"Well," he said, coming into the apartment, his face flushed with excitement, "we're off to Livermore, California!"

"To California!" Lee's eyes widened. "When?"

"They gave us two weeks before I have to report at the base. Which means we'd better get started tomorrow. It's a good long drive."

Lee was amazed at the eagerness in his voice.

"Are you—" She was still too stunned by the news to take it all in. "Rick, you sound *glad!*"

"Well, I am, kind of. I mean, it's been swell here, but it'll be sort of good to get off on our own too. I mean in a new place, making our own life, just us. Won't it?"

"Yes," Lee agreed slowly. "I guess it will, in a way." She frowned. "But, Rick, what about the apartment? And all our things, our wedding presents and everything? We can't just dash off and leave everything."

"Your mother can keep the stuff for us," Rick said sensibly. "At least until we get settled at a permanent base somewhere. Then the Air Force will ship it out to us. We'll just load the car with things we have to have—as little as we can get along with. Why don't you call your mother and ask her to take Lynda for the day so we can get packed?"

"Okay," Lee said, still doubtful. But when she was actually talking to her mother some of Rick's enthusiasm began to creep into her own voice.

"To California!" she exclaimed, delighting in her mother's little gasp of astonishment. "Leaving tomorrow! Can you imagine! Can you keep Lynda while Rick and I get all our stuff crated up?"

"Certainly," her mother said immediately. "I always love keeping Lynda. But there's no need to work yourselves to death, baby. You and I can do the packing-up leisurely after Rick has gone. You and Lynda can move in here at once, of course; but there's no reason why your things can't sit there a few days until we have a chance to get at them."

"Move back there with you?" The significance of what her mother had said came slowly. "Why?"

"Why, to stay. You won't want to live in that apartment all by yourself without Rick."

"But I'm going *with* Rick!" Lee was amazed that her mother could have thought anything else. "Didn't you hear anything I said, Mother? We're going to California. We're leaving tomorrow."

"Lee, darling"—her mother's voice was patient—"you don't know what you're talking about. Young wives don't tag around after their husbands from one training base to another, especially with small babies. It's just impossible. You and Lynda stay here

196

until Rick's through his training and stationed some-where permanently. Then you can fly out and join him. It'll be much easier on you and the baby. It's the sensible way to do things."

Lee shot Rick a quick look and shielded the telephone receiver with one hand.

"She doesn't want me to go," she whispered.

"That's too darned bad," Rick said grimly. "Whose wife are you, anyway, hers or mine?"

"Yours." Lee still hesitated. "But is it true that wives don't go along to training bases? I mean, would it be better—"

She broke off, startled by the look on Rick's face. She lowered her hand from the receiver.

"I'll bring Lynda over in a few minutes, Mother," she said quickly. "I'll talk to you then. Goodbye."

She hung up and turned back to Rick, and now, to her surprise, it was he who looked doubtful.

"You do want to come, don't you, Lee?" he asked. "I mean, it probably won't be easy to find a nice place to live right off and your mother won't be there to help you, but that doesn't matter, does it? You do want to come?"

His voice was almost pleading, and Lee felt all her love for him surge within her until it was almost too great to bear.

"Yes," she said. "I want to come. Just you try leaving me behind!"

Now her words came back to her, ringing bravely in her ears.

"Of course, I want to come!"

But I didn't know, Lee thought miserably, what it

would be like. The neighborhood and the apartment, and Rick so tired and irritable, and no diaper service, and the nasty weather, and nobody to talk to—

She stopped herself, realizing that Mrs. Dorrin was staring at her.

"I'll have to buy some soap," she said, "before I can use the washer." She waited for the woman to offer to lend her some, but wasn't surprised when she didn't. "I'll be back later," she added.

"Okay," Mrs. Dorrin agreed. "I'll be here, I guess."

When she got back to the apartment, Lee found Lynda awake and howling. She got a bottle of milk out of the refrigerator and put it in a pan of water on the stove, and while it heated and the baby screamed she made herself a peanut-butter sandwich. The sandwich and the milk were ready at the same time, and while she fed the baby and ate her sandwich she compared it to lunchtime at home, when Rick came back for lunch and they sat in the cute little rose and white breakfast room and compared the morning's events and discussed plans for the evening.

"Mother wants us to come over for dinner," Lee would say, or, "Sally called, and she and Bob are going dancing at the Glades tonight and want us to come."

It was nice having somebody to eat lunch with. On the few occasions when Rick could not get home she could always invite a girl friend over or stop for a sandwich at her mother's.

I can just see myself inviting a friend for lunch here, Lee thought bitterly, nibbling at the crust of her sandwich. "Would you like to come sit in our beautiful mustard-colored living room and eat on our lovely three-legged card table with adorable plastic spoons while Lynda shrieks bloody murder in the background? Do come—there's plenty of peanut butter for all!"

Of course, she added mentally, the only person I know to invite is Mrs. Dorrin, and I don't suppose it would matter to her. She probably thinks this is the only way to live.

Lee sighed and got up from the sofa. She carried the empty nursing bottle to the sink and rinsed it, noting as she did that now all the bottles were empty. She hesitated between making a new formula and tackling the pile of dirty diapers in the bathtub. The diapers won. She got the folding baby carriage out of the closet and, bracing herself against the cold dampness of the outside air, dragged it out the door and down the steps to the ground. Then she went back to change and dress Lynda.

The folding carriage was a parting gift from her mother. She had wheeled it out to the car just as Rick was loading the final suitcases into the back.

"If you're determined to leave the big carriage here," she had said, "at least take this with you. It'll fold down into nothing, and Lynda will be able to take her naps outside in the California sunshine."

"Huh!" Lee snorted, settling the baby in the carriage and tucking the blanket firmly around her. 'A lot we knew about California!" Nevertheless, she was extremely grateful for the carriage. The thought of carrying Lynda in her arms all the way to town and back was not a pleasant one.

"Town" was six blocks away and consisted of one street of assorted stores, one movie and a post office. The first store Lee went into carried laundry soap. She looked over the rows of boxes on the dirty shelves, selected one, paid for it, and wheeled Lynda back into the street.

Her errand done, she walked slowly, wheeling the carriage, looking in store windows. There was very little to see, but it was better than going back to the apartment. She paused at a drugstore and bought a Coke, drinking it standing up so she could keep rocking Lynda's carriage with her free hand. She leafed through the current magazines on the rack, but she found she had read most of them in the car on the drive out. Farther down the street a dress store was having a sale. There was one that was a possibility, but there was nothing to do with Lynda while she went into the tiny cubicle to try it on, so she hung it up again and wandered aimlessly out.

Lynda began to fret.

"What's the matter now?" Lee asked impatiently. She leaned over the baby and poked an inquiring finger under the blanket to feel the diaper. It was soaking.

Two more dry ones at home, she thought in sudden panic, and then she'll be all out of them!

She glanced at her watch. Four-fifteen! Barely time to put through a washing, much less get anything dry before night. Not that anything would dry in the wretched dampness anyway.

But maybe, she thought, I could hang a couple of diapers in front of the oven.

She turned the carriage and started back along the street the way she had come. As she passed the post office she hesitated and then went in.

"Do you have anything," she asked the man at the general delivery window, "for Airman or Mrs. Richard Porter?"

She had stopped completely on impulse. It was with utter amazement that she saw him turn back to her with an envelope in his hand.

"Mrs. Richard Porter," he said. "Do you have any identification?"

"Yes," Lee said eagerly. "My driver's license." She tore open her purse and hurried thumbed through her wallet until she found it.

The man studied it with maddening slowness.

"This isn't a California license," he said.

"Of course, it isn't," Lee exclaimed impatiently. "We just got to town. Please, may I have my letter?"

She practically snatched it from his hand, and immediately recognized her mother's handwriting. Now, pushing the carriage out onto the sidewalk again, she ripped it open and hungrily drew out the neat, folded pages. The paper was blue and smelled of violets. It carried the scent of the desk in her mother's bedroom, of the soft white curtains blowing at the windows, of the lavender bedspread and the cosmetics on the little cherry dressing table.

Home was suddenly so close and at the same time so far away that Lee's throat ached with the thought of it.

She unfolded the pages and began to read. "Baby . . ."

Her eyes filled with tears at the familiar endearment.

I can't believe you've been gone only a week. Since I don't have your address yet, I'm writing in hopes that you stop by the post office in Livermore. How was the trip out? I imagine it must have been a nightmare, with Lynda to take care of and the tourist courts, restaurants, and other difficulties.

Honey, I don't mean to be a fuss-budget mother, but you are so young to have the whole responsibility of a husband and baby, with no one to help you or to be within reach in emergencies. I keep thinking of all the things that could go wrong—not finding a nice place to live, having Lynda get sick, Rick's having to live on the base and seeing you only on weekends—there are so many things. I am enclosing a check to cover the plane fare home. Keep it, and if things don't go as well for you as Rick thought they would, and if you're not happy, then buy your ticket and you and Lynda come home for a while.

All my love to the three of you, darling

Mother.

The check fluttered out from between the pages, a slim yellow piece of paper. Lee caught it up, and even the sight of the bank's name printed at the top made her feel homesick.

"Oh," she whispered, "I want to go home! I want to go home—*I do!*"

The moment she allowed herself the thought, relief flooded through her in a giant wave. Why *not* go home for a little while? Until Rick got stationed somewhere permanently and could find a home in a nice neighborhood, and their wedding presents could be sent out, and Lynda was older and easier to handle and they could be really happy. Rick surely could not complain. She had given it a fair try, and after the scene this morning even Rick must realize how hopeless this sort of existence was. He wasn't happy living this way any more than she was. He was nervous and jittery and irritable, hating the apartment and worrying about his training. If he were here by himself he could live in the barracks with the other boys and concentrate on his schooling and save his pay. When they were together again everything could be perfect, the way they wanted it to be.

It'll be easier for him if I do go, Lee thought. He won't admit it at first, but after he thinks it over he will.

She began to walk quickly, pushing the carriage along ahead of her. The letter and the check were tucked safely into her purse. The stores and houses she passed were ugly and unfamiliar, but in her mind she was walking through East Orange.

Home! she thought. Soon—in a week, maybe in a couple of days—I'll be home!

Even Lynda seemed to catch the excitement, for she stopped whimpering and lay quiet in her carriage.

As they turned the corner and came in sight of the apartment, Lee felt a jolt of surprise. Their car was outside.

Why, Rick's there! she thought in confusion. What on earth is he doing there at four-thirty!

An instant later Rick was standing in front of her, his face red with fury.

"Where the devil have you been?"

Lee caught her breath. She could not remember ever seeing him so angry.

"Uptown," she said. "To buy some soap. I didn't think you'd be off work for an hour yet."

Wordlessly Rick scooped the damp baby out of the carriage and handed her to Lee and began to pull the carriage up the steps and into the apartment. Lee followed in bewilderment. Once inside, she carried Lynda into the bedroom and changed her sopping diaper. When she reentered the living room, Rick was standing by the window.

"What's the matter?" she asked softly. "What are you so angry about? I only went after soap."

He turned to her, and suddenly all the anger left his face. He caught her in his arms and he was trembling.

"Lee," he whispered, "oh, honey, I'm sorry. I didn't mean to yell. The training—it's a strain, I guess—you get so keyed up. I came home—there's a class tonight, so they let us off early this afternoon— I couldn't wait to get here and let down and be home. I came in, and you weren't here! I couldn't imagine what happened to you. I was so darned scared. This neighborhood—I know it's not a nice one, and I'd left you alone here and now you were gone! Oh, honey, if anything happened to you—"

His voice broke and he stopped talking. He just clung to her, young and shaken and oddly helpless.

Why, he needs me! Lee thought in amazement. He doesn't just love me—he needs me too! He needs me here when he comes home!

It was such a new thought that it was difficult to take in—the fact that a strong, slightly bossy young husband could need her as much as—probably more than—she needed him.

Lee reached up and pushed back the curly dark hair which was so much like Lynda's. She heard herself saying, "Hey, I'm a grown woman now, remember? I've got a husband and a daughter. You don't have to worry about me. I can take care of myself."

As though she were listening to someone else she heard her own voice, light, warm, soothing, very sure and confident. It reminded her of her mother's voice when something had gone wrong.

"I was crazy," Rick said brokenly, "to ask you to come out here. As soon as my first paycheck comes in, you're going back. Why, they'll probably ship me to another base in a couple of weeks, and you'd have to get things set to move all over again!"

"Don't be silly," Lee said. She was amused to hear herself using all the arguments she had been prepared to combat. "Moving's kind of fun, really."

"The lousy apartments—"

"There's nothing wrong with this apartment."

"There's no room—"

"There's plenty of room."

"And it's hard on the baby—"

"The baby will do just fine," Lee said. "She'll learn to get along just like we do. It'll be a grand experience for the baby."

I am a grown woman, she thought, remembering her own words. My husband needs me.

She felt suddenly calmer, older, more confident than she had ever been before.

"When I came in," Rick whispered, "and you weren't here, the place was so empty. I didn't think I could stand it."

In the bedroom Lynda started to scream for supper. Her voice got louder and angrier, and Lee remembered that she had not made the formula or bought any strained pears and that it was too late to get a laundry done. In the bathtub was the pile of dirty diapers, there were suitcases still to be unpacked in the bedroom, dinner was not yet started, and there was a bag of garbage in the corner of the living room.

But they were only minor crises. They might panic a bride, not a wife.

"It's funny," Lee said softly, still in Rick's arms "but even if you're just gone a couple of hours, it's always a good feeling to get home."

She glanced around the apartment, and it was not really too terrible. In fact, the sunlight was slanting in through the windows, and the mustard-colored walls, which were so horrible in the morning, softened and glowed almost golden in the late-afternoon light.

14

When "home to mother" appeared in print, I was suddenly flooded with mail. Young wives from all over the country wrote to say, "Yes, I know! That's exactly the way it is! I thought something must be wrong with me, that I should feel this way. It's such a relief to know that I am not alone!" There were at least a dozen letters from women married to servicemen who had been stationed at Livermore. They recognized the description of the town with its one block of dreary little stores, and one girl wrote, "I know that apartment! It's the same one *we* rented, and they still haven't painted the walls!"

I received only one letter from a man. It was from Arnold, my friend from my sophomore year in high school. We had lost track of each other over the years, and he wrote me now in care of *McCalls*. He was in medical school, and his wife subscribed to the magazine.

"Mary and I both read your painful and beautiful story," he wrote. "It all reads true except for the ending. That's a fake, like your old music article; you created that in order to sell the story."

Along with these letters from readers, I received three letters from literary agents asking if they could represent me.

In writers' magazines, I had read about agents. They are people who market a writer's work in return for a percentage of her earnings. Editors are more receptive to manuscripts that are given them by agents, because they know that an agent will not represent someone he does not think is good. An agent is also knowledgeable about marketing secondary rights to a writer's work, and will often be able to sell foreign rights to other countries and theatrical rights to television or to the movies.

I was thrilled to think that my sale to such a large-circulation magazine would boost my reputation to such a point that agents would be interested in me. I was also bewildered as to what to do about it. I knew that some agents were supposed to be better than others, and the names of the three who had written meant nothing to me. Was one superior to the others? How should I choose?

I finally decided to write the fiction editor of *McCalls* and ask her opinion. Her answer was immediate and helpful. She advised me to reject all three of them. "The best agents have writers banging on their doors, begging to be represented," she told me. "They don't need to go out soliciting. If you are interested in acquiring an agent, I suggest you write to one of the following," and she gave me several names and addresses as well as her own personal letter of recommendation. I gratefully did as instructed and two of the agents responded favorably. The one I finally selected seemed right for several reasons. For one thing, she represented some very well-known authors such as John Steinbeck and Patrick Dennis. For another, she was willing to market juveniles, which the other agent was not. The first thing she did for me was to sell foreign rights to "Home to Mother" in England, Sweden, South Africa, and Germany. I was so impressed that I hurriedly finished up my college book and sent the manuscript of that to her.

By this time it was Christmas—quite a lovely Christmas, I thought, because we had a home of our own to celebrate in and two little girls to tear open presents. Also, for the first time in two years, we were able to share the holiday with my parents. The one missing person was my brother. Bill was now in the Air Force, stationed in New Mexico. Having a family Christmas without Bill was strange. He had been only sixteen when Buzz and I were married, and though he had grown up and graduated and was now an adult with a life of his own, I still thought of him as my "little brother."

One of the presents I sent him that year was "from the Moon Fairy" whom I had created for him during childhood. And I wrote a story about a brother and sister who had grown apart for a while and then found each other again.

The Lost Christmas
written at age 22,
published in American Girl, *December 1962*

"Brice, will you give me a ride uptown?"

"Nope, I'm busy."

"Then may I use your car? It won't take long; I just have to pick up my new formal before the store closes."

"Are you crazy? You know I never lend my car to anybody." Brice glanced up from the paper on which he was scribbling. "I'm totaling up tomorrow night's expenses—tickets, corsage, food after the dance. I hope Midge sticks to a Coke and a hamburger."

"From what I hear, she's the type to order pheasant under glass." I tried to sound beguiling. "Please, Brice—the snow has turned to slush, and I don't want to have to hike to the bus and back. It's Christmas Eve—why not show a little brotherly love?"

Brice sighed and laid the paper aside. "It doesn't feel much like Christmas this year. As far as I'm concerned, it's kind of turned into nothing. Maybe we've outgrown it or something."

"No," I said. "It's not that. It's that Mother isn't here."

I don't think any of us had realized before how

important Mother's warmth and enthusiasm were in binding our family together—not until this year when she was spending the holidays with Grandma, who was ill. Suddenly, it was as though there were no Christmas at all. Dad had driven Mother to Grandmother's and returned to immerse himself in his business affairs; at home Brice and I had very little to say to each other.

Mother had been gone for a week, and we had been too occupied with our own affairs and the unaccustomed daily housekeeping to think about the coming holiday. Dad had bought a tree—a lopsided little fir because the good ones had been picked over by the time he reached the lot—and I had decorated it. It sat now in the corner of the living room, overloaded with ornaments and already beginning to shed its needles.

"At least there's the dance," I said. "That should be fun, and I *have* to get my formal. It's my one big Christmas present from Mother and Daddy, the way the seat belts in your car were for you. The Jennings Shop had to order it specially from its New York store because they didn't have a blue one in stock, and they phoned today to tell me it has come. Please, Brice—they close early Christmas Eve."

"Oh, all right," Brice said impatiently. "Sometimes I envy guys who don't have sisters. At least, they don't have to act as private taxi services."

He stood up, holding himself very straight, trying to stretch a couple of extra inches onto his height. Although Brice is a senior, he is only two inches taller than I am. But he is a nice-looking boy, with curly hair and very blue eyes and a nice smile—when he smiles.

He was not smiling now. "Come on," he said, and we went into the hall to put on our coats and out the kitchen way to the garage.

We have a double garage. In one side Daddy keeps his station wagon, and Brice has taken the other for his car. Brice started saving for that car when he was twelve years old and Uncle Richard gave him five dollars for his birthday.

"I'm putting it in the bank," he announced immediately, "to save for my car." And the very next day he had Dad go down with him while he opened a savings account. From then on, half of his allowance and every extra dollar he earned at summer jobs went into his car fund. The week after he turned sixteen he bought the car.

"It's secondhand, of course," he said, "but it's in great condition. Take a look at that engine!"

He raised the hood, and we all looked inside while he pointed out wires and hoses and little black plugs with grease on them. I think we were all amazed that he knew so much about what went on inside an engine.

Mother said, "That's wonderful, dear—just wonderful," but later, after Brice had left to take the car to show to some friends, she had asked Dad, "Do you think we should let him have it? He seems so terribly young still," and Dad had answered, "There's not much we can do about it. He paid for the thing himself, you know."

So the car moved into the garage next to Dad's,

and Dad said sometimes that he was ashamed to see them there together, because Brice's was always so brightly polished.

Now, however, as we walked over to it, I had the funny feeling that the car, like the little Christmas tree, was a trifle lopsided.

I said, "What's the matter with it?"

"The matter?" Brice had been opening the garage doors, and now he turned in alarm. "What do you mean?"

"It sits lower on one side than on the other."

"You're crazy," Brice said. "It couldn't—" And then he stopped. In a few quick steps he reached the far side of the car. "Oh, gosh, you're right, the tire's flat! It's not only flat, it's finished—it's slashed right through the sidewall! It must have hit against a rock or something!"

"Oh, dear." I glanced at my watch. "How long will it take you to change it?"

There was a moment's silence. When Brice spoke again there was an odd note in his voice. "I can't change it."

"Why not? You have a jack, don't you? Why can't you just put on the spare?"

"I—I don't have a spare. Not anymore." He stood gazing down at it. "I sold my spare to Scotty Nolan."

"You *sold* it!"

"Yes. I had spent all my cash on Christmas presents, and then Midge said she'd go with me to the formal—I never thought she'd do it—and I had to have money for the ticket and the corsage—" His voice faded off.

214

"And you've been driving without a spare for weeks now!" I exclaimed reprovingly. "Dad will have a fit."

"Well, go ahead and tell him, Miss Tattleblabber. That's the least of my worries. This finishes off my date with Midge for tomorrow."

"Why, Brice, that's ridiculous," I said. "You can always ride over with Dick and me. Dick's uncle is going to drive us and pick us up after. There'll be plenty of room."

"Thanks, but no thanks," Brice said shortly.

"Why? Are you so embarrassed by your kid sister that you don't want your precious Midge to be exposed to—"

"Oh, come off it, Connie. It's not anything like that, and you know it. It's just that—that—" His voice was low and shaky.

Suddenly, to my surprise, the toughness was gone from his face; it looked young and vulnerable the way it had a long time ago when we were children. "How do you suppose I got a date with Midge in the first place? Do you really think a girl as pretty and popular as she is would date a—a shrimp like me—when she could be going with a dozen other taller guys? It's the car that's doing it. I'm one of the few seniors with his own car to take her in."

"For goodness sake, Brice," I said in astonishment, "how can you want to date her if she's like that?"

"Because, she's—she's—" His face was bright red. "Well, why do you like Dick so much? He's not so red-hot that I can see, just kind of dumb and ordinary, but you can't help it, you just want to go out with him. And that's how I am about Midge. I thought maybe if she dated me a few times and got a chance to know me better, she might have fun—I mean, she'd see that just being short doesn't mean a guy's not worth going with, and then she'd like me for me—without the car even—" He was stumbling along miserably when he seemed to remember to whom he was talking. He cleared his throat, and when he spoke again the old cockiness was back in his voice. "Oh, what's the difference? There'll be lots of other dances. You'd better get going if you want to make it to the bus stop."

The bus was just pulling up to the corner when I reached it. I ran the last few yards and stumbled up the steps into the warm interior. Dropping my change into the slot, I made my way to the back and sank into the only empty seat. Then I relaxed and leaned back to look about me. The bus was crowded with people laughing and talking, clutching bags and boxes and odd-shaped parcels. The woman in the next seat had an armload of Christmas wreaths, and their piny odor drifted back to me in a wave of spicy sweetness. Behind me, two children, a boy and a girl, were giggling together over a package they had precariously balanced on the seat between them, and every few minutes one of them would peek inside to see that whatever it contained was still there.

Glancing back at them, I felt a wave of nostalgia, for they reminded me so much of Brice and me at that age. We had been inseparable then, riding our bicycles and building clubhouses, hiding treasures, and sharing secrets.

"I'm glad my children are so close in age," Mother had said one time, "for they are such wonderful companions. No matter what happens during their lives, they will always have each other to fall back on."

Remembering the words now, I was filled with a strange, empty sense of loss. What, I asked myself in bewilderment, had happened? The friendship, the closeness, the fun and companionship we had shared, where had they gone? Somehow, during the past few years they had vanished. Brice had gone his way and I mine. With Mother at home, it had not been so noticeable—her love for both of us had seemed to draw the family together. But now, in her absence, the truth became apparent. Brice and I had found our separate friends, our separate interests; we were pulling apart in different directions. The brother I had once known so well had become to me almost a stranger—aloof and cocky and superior, irritated by and scornful of everything I did and said.

Almost a stranger, and yet—not quite. I remembered his face as I had seen it in the garage—a face gone young with misery. There had been nothing superior about it then.

The bus had reached town now and was pulling up to the corner in front of the Jennings Shop. I got up. The two children behind me were still giggling together as I started down the aisle to the door.

Clutching my purse, I clambered down the steps to the sidewalk, knowing what I had to do.

The saleslady in the Jennings Shop looked up with a smile as I came in. "Hello, can I help you?"

"Yes," I said, "I want to return a dress."

"To return—" She glanced at my empty arms. "Do you have it with you?"

"No," I said, "it's already here—the name is Connie Parker. It's a formal ankle-length taffeta, like the pink one in the front window, only in blue. Mother ordered it for me as a Christmas present."

"I see." The girl looked puzzled. "Then you have decided you don't want the dress after all?"

"That's right. Mother has already paid you. I would like the money refunded instead."

"This is rather irregular. I'll have to speak to the manager. Will you wait a minute please?" The girl disappeared into a back room. When she reappeared a few moments later she was carrying a box with a slip of paper attached to it. "I can refund the money if you want me to. It does seem a shame—the dress is lovely. Wouldn't you like to look at it before you decide?"

"No, thank you," I said. "I'll just take the money, please."

I forced my eyes away from the box. I knew perfectly well that it was a lovely dress. I knew what it would do for me too, the shimmering ice blue—that it would put blond highlights into my hair and make my eyes larger and bluer. I had hoped that when Dick saw me in it I would seem different to him—not just a pleasant girl to take occasionally to

dances but someone rather special. I had hoped . . .
but I had a party dress at home, several years old
and a little bit weary, but perfectly wearable even to
a Christmas dance.

"I'll just take the money," I said again, and when it
was in my purse I left quickly.

At a garage two blocks away I bought the tire. I
did not know a thing about tires, and I did not know
exactly what to ask for.

"I don't know what size," I said, naming the car.
"But it's a fifty-seven two-door hardtop."

"What kind of tire?" the man asked me. "Tube or
tubeless?"

"I—I don't know." It sounded like another language. "Is there a difference?"

"Yes," the man said gently, "there's a difference.
Since it's a fifty-seven, I think you'd better take the
tube too."

"All right," I agreed.

He went into the back of the garage and came
back with a tire and a small, flat box. "Here you are,"
he said, glancing around. "Where do you want me to
put it? Is somebody picking you up here?"

"No," I said. "I'm going on the bus."

"Lady," he said, "you can't do it—not with the
Christmas crowds. They wouldn't let you on."

"I guess you're right." I counted out the money,
seeing to my relief that there were a few dollars
remaining from the price of the dress. "I guess
maybe I'd better take a taxi."

Brice was out front, shoveling at the snow in the
driveway, when the cab pulled up in front of the

house. Dropping the shovel, he came to the curb to meet me.

"Good gosh," he said when he saw the tire. "Where did you get that?"

"At a garage," I said snappishly. "Where else?"

"But what are you doing with it?"

"Giving it to you." I rolled it to him. It wobbled lopsidedly across the snow and he put out his hand and caught it. He kept staring at it as though he didn't believe it was real.

"Go jack it on," I said, "or whatever you do. It's your Christmas present."

Brice was silent a moment. Then he said, "I thought we agreed we weren't going to give presents to each other this year. We were going to use our money to get extra nice things for Mother and Grandmother."

"All right," I said, "so I broke the agreement. Can't a girl change her mind without your making a federal case of it?" Suddenly I was so irritated that I felt like slapping him. "Now you can take your precious Midge to the dance in style. You might at least say thank you."

"Well, sure," Brice said gruffly. "Thanks." He opened his mouth as though he were going to say something more and then he closed it again.

"You're welcome," I said and went past him into the house.

Standing in the hallway, taking off my coat and galoshes, my eyes blurred with the hot sting of tears. I blinked them back angrily, asking myself just what it was that I had expected. Did I think Brice was going to fall to his knees in gratitude? Did I expect him to throw his arms around me and hug me— Brice who had stopped hugging Mother by the time he was twelve years old?

No, I answered myself honestly, what I had wanted was even greater. I had hoped to be able to go back eight years with one great leap and have us friends again, close friends the way we used to be. But things did not work that way. You could not pull closed a gap between people with a tire and a tube—not when the people had grown as far apart as we had.

Next day we drove with Dad to Grandmother's. Mother met us at the door. Dad and Brice and I gave her her presents, watching her face light up with love and pleasure as she untied the ribbons. Dad had a beautiful housecoat and a new charm for her bracelet, and Brice gave her earrings and perfume, and I had spent every cent of my gift money on a white and gold evening bag.

"It's beautiful!" Mother gasped when she saw it, and she drew my face down and kissed me. "Everything is so beautiful! I'm so lucky to have such a wonderful family!" And again I found my eyes filling with tears.

Grandmother was better, Mother told us. Grandfather took us up to see her for a few moments. She looked small and frail in the big bed, but her hair was beautifully dressed as usual and her smile was as gay as ever.

The house, when we got home again, seemed cold and empty. Dad parked the car while Brice and I went in ahead of him and turned on the lights. I stopped in the living room and looked at the lop-sided little tree, drooping sadly under the weight of its ornaments, and wondered why I had ever bothered decorating it in the first place. Brice had said that we had outgrown Christmas, and I thought now that he was right. Christmas was gone, a part of the fun of childhood, and we could never bring it back again.

The electric cord hung limply down one side of the tree, and on impulse I reached down and plugged it in. The lights sprang on in an array of colors, and their soft glow showed me beneath the tree a square flat package. I knelt down and picked it up. It had not been there that afternoon, I was certain. The card on it said, "Merry Christmas to Connie."

I stared at it in amazement. Then slowly and carefully I began to remove the wrappings. The box itself was so light that I could not believe there was anything in it. When I lifted the top, I saw that my guess was not a bad one, for all that was inside was a sheet of white paper on which was pasted a picture from a magazine. It had been torn partway through—the front hood and bumper of a car.

"What in the world . . ."

"It's one third," Brice said. I raised my eyes, and he was standing there, looking down at me. "One third interest in the car."

"You mean—" I could not believe my ears.

"One third interest," he said again. "That means that you can use it a third of the time, for club meetings and to go uptown and things like that. Or just to ride around in."

"Why, Brice—" I said. "Brice—"

For one brief moment, looking into his eyes, I saw reflected there all the things that were in my own, the things that I had thought to keep so carefully hidden: the problems and worries and dreams and fears that make growing up so difficult for a girl—or for a boy. I saw something else there too, wedged down deep beneath the layers and layers of protective covering, clear and bright and unmistakable—the look of love.

"Well, after all," he said, "You *are* my sister." He shifted in sudden embarrassment, and the old gruffness came back into his voice. "Of course, you'll have to pay for your share of the gas."

"Of course," I said.

In the soft glow of the tree lights, the room was filled with Christmas. It had been there all the time.

Many years later, when my own children were teenagers, the fiction editor of *Good Housekeeping* wrote to tell me they were putting together their December issue and needed a short-short story of approximately one thousand words. Did I have something to submit to them?

As I went through my files, I came across "The Lost Christmas."

So much time had passed since the writing of this story that I sat and read it with the feeling that it had been written by someone else. I could not even remember the ending. When I finished it, I thought, Now, that's not a bad plot. I bet *Good Housekeeping* would like it.

Of course, I couldn't sell the story over again. *American Girl* had bought all rights. Besides, *Good Housekeeping* will not take reprints, and their viewpoint characters are seldom teenagers.

But an *idea* cannot be copyrighted. It is the property of anyone who wants it. I took the idea behind this story and used it again. The new story was written in third person instead of first, from the viewpoint of Susan, a mother who is heartsick over the fact that her teenage children, once so close, now spar like prizefighters. In this new story, Susan's daughter has accepted a babysitting job for New Year's Eve and is then invited out that evening by the boy of her dreams. Her brother, who has announced that he can't afford to give presents this year, slips a "pencil-thin package tied with bright red ribbon" under the tree.

His mother asks him if this is some kind of a joke:

"Not exactly." Brad looked embarrassed. "It's an IOU for New Year's Eve. I'm going to take Lynda's place babysitting." He ducked his head, avoiding his mother's eyes. "Heck, I might as well. I'm not doing anything anyway."

In the den the stereo burst into a wild blast. The telephone began to ring. As he went to answer it, Brad reached out and flicked on the television.

"Merry Christmas," said Susan.

She could not hear the words for the noise, but she did not have to hear them. Their magic rose and filled the room, soft as a snowflake, holy as a star.

The first story brought me $75. The second brought me $1,500.

It was lucky I learned early in life that a professional writer always keeps carbons.

🌿 15

I DID NOT KEEP A DIARY during the early years of my marriage, but I did continue to keep a poetry notebook, which reflects the thoughts and emotions of that time.

Mother to Be
written at age 20

All these years, and I never knew!
Time after time I have passed this way
When the world was soft as it is today,
And I never saw that the sky was blue—
Never noticed the daisy faces
Laughing up from hidden places,
Silly and golden, scattered along.
All these years I have seen spring come,
And I never listened and heard a song,
Never noticed the busy hum
Of a sleepy world that is yawning and waking
With green things stretching and hard buds breaking.
Year after year there has been a spring.

Always before I have stood apart
And watched her come, but now I sing,
And the world is a bursting, blooming thing,
And I have a secret under my heart!

The Faithful Wife
written at age 21

Oh, it's many a mile and it's many a mile
To the wondrous land of Spain,
But I have stood on a Spanish hill
And laughed in the silver rain.
I have crouched in a Spanish fort
And heard the cannons roar,
And spent the night 'neath crimson sheets
In the arms of a matador.

Oh, it's many a mile and it's many a mile
To the splendid China wall.
But I have eaten toasted snails
And slept in a silken shawl.
I have listened to peacocks scream
And watched the coolies flee,
And found my love with a Chinese prince
In the shade of a mulberry tree.

Oh, it's many a mile from our kitchen door
To half the world away.
I lie at night in the curve of your arm
And I cook your meals by day.
All of my life I give to you
And glad that it may be so—

But my heart goes roaming many a mile
That you will never know.

Woman Alone
written at age 22,
published in Good Housekeeping, *April* 1971

The night is long with you away.
The wind is loud in the maple tree,
And something rustles against the door
    Where no sound should be.

A creaking such as a shutter makes
Sounds, though the shutters are bolted tight,
And footsteps brush on the empty stair,
    Loud in the night.

The bed is large and strange and cold
And sleep is fragile as a song.
When you were here I never knew
    Night was so long.

I had married anticipating the same sort of easy companionship my parents enjoyed, but I did not find it. Buzz was seldom home except to sleep. Nights he spent "at the library" or "relaxing with the guys," while on weekends he was gone fishing, snorkeling and waterskiing. For me to accompany him meant hiring a sitter, which we couldn't afford. On the few occasions I did splurge in this manner, Buzz seemed less overjoyed than irritated.

The fault must be mine, I decided. I had "let myself go." There must be ways I could make myself more interesting and desirable. I started my self-improvement campaign by joining a Great Books club to stimulate my mind and doing daily sit-ups to flatten my stomach. I experimented with exotic new recipes, bought a lacy black negligee, and bleached my dishwater-blond hair buttercup yellow. (The result of this last venture was that the hair began coming out by the handful and clogged the shower drain so badly we had a forty-dollar plumbing bill.) To broaden myself as a person, I took up photography, and found to my amazement that I enjoyed it tremendously. Growing up in a photographers' household, I had unconsciously absorbed a good deal of knowledge about technique and composition, and before long I was taking good enough pictures to use as illustrations for some of my articles. I also discovered that photography was one way of coping with my visual memory problem. If I lined a scene up in the viewfinder of a camera, I remembered it! Not the scene itself, but the camera image. And with the photographic print to reinforce my memory, I could actually absorb a person's features so well that I knew who he was the next time I saw him.

To fill the long evenings after the little girls were in bed, I began work on another novel. The idea for this book came to me when I read a notice on the society page of my hometown newspaper listing a schedule of events for "this season's debutantes." I was incredulous. The one high school had such a small student body that when I had attended there had been no dividing line between students from well-to-do families and those from poorer ones. We had all gone around together, and popularity was based upon personality rather than social background.

What a sad season, I thought, for a girl whose friends were chosen to be "debs," but who herself was excluded from all the dances and parties. How might such a girl be affected by this experience? How would she be changed as a person?

I fashioned the girl after myself, named her Lynn, and placed her in the familiar setting of my own high school years. The town was Sarasota, renamed Rivertown. Although I myself had never experienced the mad whirl of the debutante social season, my brother had. Bill had been a senior the year the deb program had been established and had been drafted as escort for one of the girls. Because of this, and because they had been chaperons at some of the parties, my parents were able to give me a detailed description of what they had been like. Through talking with them and with some of the debs themselves, most of whom were younger sisters of my former classmates, I could draw a fairly realistic picture of a situation I was glad I had not had to be involved in.

My practice on the previous book-length manuscript had given me an idea of how to pace the action chapter by chapter, and I really enjoyed having a continuing project that I could pick up and work on during empty hours the way other people might their knitting.

I finished typing the final draft of *Debutante Hill* the same week that Buzz took the Florida Bar exam, and mailed it off to my agent with a note suggesting that she enter it in a contest I had read about in a magazine. She acknowledged this with a note saying it would be a waste of effort, as the contest was a national one and thousands of experienced professional writers from all over the country would be entering. I wrote back asking her to enter it anyway. What was there to lose but some postage? Nothing had happened with my college book, so I really had little hope for this one. I just liked the idea of having some control over where it would be submitted.

Buzz had done well in school and had no doubts about having passed the Bar, so he began a series of interviews with firms around the state of Florida. With my book finished and out of my hands, I looked restlessly around for another project. It was a relief to have one handed to me. The fiction editor of *Seventeen* wrote asking if I had a story on file about the relationship between two sisters.

I didn't, but I agreed to write one.

Back in my grammar-school days, I had ridden the school bus with a girl named Martha Dunning. Dunning wasn't her last name; it went with the

Martha. People called her Martha Dunning when they spoke to her. I was horrified by the idea of being known by such a mouthful, and once I timidly asked her how she felt about it. She told me it was a family name and she was used to it, and then added, after a short pause, "You should hear what our folks named my sister."

I didn't have the nerve to ask her, and I'd wondered about it ever since. Was the sister's name longer or shorter? Prettier or uglier? The question had hung dormant in the back of my mind for over twelve years. Now it came popping forth to give me a jump-off point for a story.

I did not know it then, but this was to be the last teenage short story that I would write.

April
written at age 23,
published in Seventeen *October 1957*

My sister's name is April. She was born in the spring. Mother says it was the first real day of spring when the air was suddenly warm and soft and fresh and dandelions popped out on the lawn and the first group of birds invaded the birdbath in the backyard. Mother isn't usually the romantic type, but when she heard the birds and felt springtime pouring in the open window she completely forgot the baby was to be named Martha Dunning after an aunt.

She said, "Her name is April."

So when I came along a year later, the Martha

Dunning name was still lying around waiting to be used. I was born in the hottest part of August, so there was no inspiration for anything else.

I've often wondered whether, if things had been different—if I had been the springtime baby and April had come in dead summer and been Martha Dunning—maybe we would have been different people too. I've wondered how much being named April had to do with making April look like springtime. Because she does. Even when we were very little, people would look at April with her soft, light hair shining silver over her shoulders and her eyes a dark, dark blue, almost a purple blueness, and smile. As she grew older the loveliness did not fade the way it does with so many pretty children. If anything, she grew more beautiful each day.

Sometimes I would catch Mother and Daddy looking at her and then glancing at each other and shaking their heads as though to say, "How in the world did we—two quite average people—ever produce anything like this!" And aside from being exquisite to look at, April is sweet. It is a gentle, childlike sweetness that makes her like and trust everybody, and when she was little, Mother and Daddy were fiercely protective. Although she was the older, I always felt as though she were my younger sister, and in all our games I was the one who led and made the rules. She was a year ahead of me in school, but it was I who taught her to read, carefully pointing out the letters and pronouncing the words.

"Oh, Martha," April would sigh, staring at the

page in bewilderment, "I'll never be able to do it. All those letters making words and the words making sense . . . How do you ever remember what they all are! I'm so dumb!"

"No," I would say quickly, "of course, you're not dumb, April. You'll learn. It just takes time."

"But look at you!" April would exclaim. "You've been able to read practically since you were a baby!"

Which was true. I loved books with a passionate devotion, and the problems of reading never held any terrors for me.

"Oh, some people are good at some things," I would say, "and some at others. Come on and try again."

At last she did learn to read, at least well enough to get by, but she never liked it. I don't believe I have ever seen April pick up a book for pleasure. And then came a worse step—multiplication tables—and then long division and fractions and algebra, and finally Latin and biology and chemistry. Through them all, April struggled earnestly, and I spent hours with her at home, and finally, when our report cards came, she would produce D's and C's, and Mother and Daddy would always say, "Well, that's fine, dear."

And to my straight A's they would say, "That's fine, dear," in exactly the same tone of voice. And April would smile with such radiant relief that they would kiss her impulsively. Because, after all, she did try so hard and was so beautiful.

Our house was a good-sized one and April and I each had her own room. April's room was the smaller, but it had a window overlooking the back-yard garden and in summer it always smelled of flowers and freshly cut grass. It was done in pink and white with fluffy curtains at the windows and a dressing table with a ruffle around it covered with pink rosebuds. My room was yellow and brown, with a chocolate rug and sunny curtains and several rows of bookshelves and a large desk. The rooms were as different as we were, but they were both nice in their own ways.

"Your room looks so comfortable in winter," April would say, wandering in to toss herself across the foot of the bed where I lay reading. "I think it's the yellow—it seems so warm and friendly."

"Well, you can spend the winter with me," I would answer, "and I'll come visit your room in the spring."

Then we would both laugh, for we knew how hopeless our sharing a room would be—like trying to mix orange sherbet with mashed potatotes.

I liked my room. It suited me, and there was plenty of room for the books I loved so much and for my desk, which would never have fitted into April's room. Even so, sometimes I would pass her door and glance in and see the fluff of curtains and the rosebud dressing table, and I would wonder what it would be like to have such a dainty room and to fit in it as perfectly as April did.

We both had our boys. April, of course, had admirers in droves from the time she started kinder-garten, and by the time she reached high school she never had a choice of less than three or four invitations to the school dances. I went to the dances too, although my admirers seemed to consist of only one boy at a time. I was never actually jealous, because April whisked back and forth from one boy to another so gaily that it made it all seem like a game.

Until the arrival of Jeff Reigle.

Jeff was much older than the boys we were used to dating. We would never have known him at all if Daddy had not been introduced to him at Rotary. He was a fine young man, Daddy told us, in business for himself, and Daddy had invited him over to visit.

"April's a senior now—eighteen years old," he told us. "It's time she met somebody besides the high school crowd."

"How old is he?" we asked in amazement. Daddy had always been so strict about our dating boys our own age.

"Oh, twenty-five or twenty-six," Daddy said slowly.

April and I were stunned. "Ancient!" we whispered to each other.

But when Jeff arrived he was not ancient at all. Nor was he handsome. He was tall and sturdy with a square, stubborn chin, and he was wearing a slightly surly expression, as though he were not in the least happy about being dragged to meet a couple of high school girls. But there was something about him—a strength and maturity—that was very attractive.

"—my daughters . . ." Daddy was saying, "April and Martha Dunning."

Jeff nodded politely to April and then to me, and

then his eyes shifted back to April, and the sullen expression left his face. Instead there came into his eyes the look that boys always got when they looked at April. I had never minded before, but now suddenly I felt a sudden heaviness in the pit of my stomach.

He said, "How do you do, Martha Dunning . . . April . . ." and his voice lingered on the "April" as though surprised at how well the name fitted the girl. I thought what a perfectly ghastly name Martha Dunning was in comparison.

April smiled. Her smile is wonderful, like a flood of sunlight. She always smiles at everybody, but anyone on the receiving end is always absolutely sure that she has been waiting her whole lifetime just to smile at him.

I don't remember exactly what we talked about that evening. I know that Jeff was wonderfully polite; he divided his attention equally between us. He asked me if I liked sports and where I wanted to go to college and what books I read. He even seemed to be interested in my answers, but then his eyes would wander back to April.

After Jeff left and April and I were upstairs getting ready for bed, I tried to think of some way to bring the conversation around to Jeff, but I did not have to for April mentioned him herself.

"He's nice, isn't he?" she said dreamily. "Jeff Reigle, I mean."

"Yes." I glanced sideways at her standing in front of my mirror, brushing her hair.

"He asked me for a date," she said. "When he was saying good night. For this Friday. I think it should be fun, don't you?"

I nodded, feeling my throat tighten.

"You have a date Friday night too, don't you, Martha?"

"Yes," I said. "I do." It was with Timmy Kendal, one of the boys in my class. Timmy was pleasant and I had been looking forward to the evening, but now suddenly I didn't think I could bear to have Friday come.

As it happened, Timmy arrived early, so I never got to see Jeff. We got home around eleven-thirty and I said a hurried good night and went upstairs. April was not home yet. I went to my room and set my hair and got ready for bed and tried to settle down to read, but I could not concentrate. It was almost one o'clock before I heard the tap of April's feet in the hall.

She hesitated by my door, saw the light, and came in.

She was wearing a green dress that swished about her like spring breezes and her hair was rippling silver across her shoulders. She smiled at me, and I knew how she must have looked to Jeff.

I said, "Hi. Did you have a nice time?"

"Oh, yes," breathed April. "It was marvelous! We had dinner on the terrace of the San Carlos Hotel. There was dancing, and there's nothing but sky over you up there and when you look down off the edge you can see lights all the way down to the river."

"What's Jeff like?" I asked, trying to keep my voice casual.

"Jeff? Oh, Martha," and her voice was singing in a way I had never heard before, "Martha, he's wonderful! He's not like anybody I've ever known! He treated me like . . . as if I was going to break any minute . . . and he thinks I'm beautiful!"

She said it with such wonder and joy that I was able to keep my resentment out of my voice.

"Of course he does," I said. "Because you are. You're innocent and sweet and springtime. You're" —I managed to smile—"you're April."

April smiled too, not really understanding.

"Well, of course, I'm April," she said. "And you're Martha. And you must have had quite an evening yourself to be talking like such a nut! Good night."

After she was gone I lay there for a long time, thinking. April was beautiful and unspoiled, but was that really enough? Oh, for the high school boys, yes. But Jeff Reigle was a grown man with his school days far behind him, established in his own business, used to adult companionship. What really did he and April have to talk about? April was never tongue-tied—she could chatter gaily along about school and parties and movie stars, but surely after a while this could become boring to a man like Jeff. I, on the other hand, had read so much; I had opinions on so many things that school boys shrugged off as silly, but things a man would respond to and find interesting.

It wouldn't hurt to try anyway, I thought defensively. After all, April had so many boys in love with her, and Jeff Reigle was the first man I'd ever felt this way about. If I could get him interested in me intellectually, surely it wouldn't hurt April . . .

I don't know, thinking back on it, if my plan would have worked. Sometimes I think it would have; other times I don't. There were occasions, I know, there in the beginning before their love was established and final when Jeff did seem a little bored with April's chatter. I tried to make the most of these opportunities. I would ask Jeff something about a book we'd both read—about art or politics or philosophy—something that would leave April out of the conversation or would cause her to make some remark to show her ignorance. And Jeff would be interested. He liked stimulating conversation, and he would turn to me eagerly.

April didn't know what was going on. She is never suspicious of anyone, least of all me.

Mother, however, is not gullible. She drew me aside one day and said quietly, "Martha Dunning, I know what you are doing, or trying to do, and I don't want to see any more of it."

"What do you mean?" I asked, a little frightened by Mother's tone of voice.

"Jeff," she said decidedly, "is April's beau. He is right for April; he is old enough and strong enough to take care of her the way your father and I have always done. I don't want you spoiling things for them, Martha Dunning."

"But, Mother," I gasped in amazement. "You sound as though you want them to get married."

"Well," Mother said thoughtfully, "Jeff would make April a good husband."

At first I was too stunned to reply. Finally I said, "What about me? Don't you care about my having a good husband too?"

"Oh, for goodness sake," said Mother impatiently, "you just think you care for Jeff because he's the first mature man you've known. You'll find somebody at college or afterward; you have all the time in the world, Martha Dunning."

And that, of course, was the end of my plan.

Jeff and April were married that spring right after April's graduation. The wedding was in the little church two blocks over, and we had the reception in the garden afterward, and people said it was the loveliest they had ever seen. April looked like an angel drifting down the aisle in her wedding gown with her hair shimmering in the sunlight that flowed through the open windows, and afterward when she threw back her veil and lifted her radiant face to Jeff's, there wasn't a person in the church who did not catch his breath.

I glanced across at Mother and Daddy, and they were standing very close together, hand in hand, watching her with a glow on their faces that nearly matched her own. And standing there in my new pink gown, I thought resentfully, Why did April have to insist on her maid of honor's wearing pink when she knew yellow was my best color? I felt a surge of bitterness toward April for being so beautiful and toward Jeff for marrying her, and toward Mother and Daddy for loving her so much. It was an ugly feeling. I knew it, and I was ashamed of it, but I could not drive it away.

There was one moment during the reception when I almost lost it. It was when April flew up to me, her face glowing, and impulsively seized my hands and said in that soft sweet way of hers, "Oh, Martha, I only hope you're as happy on your wedding day as I am now!"

I squeezed her hands and said, "You deserve to be happy, honey." But then, as she turned away, the envy returned in a vicious surge because I saw Mother standing by the buffet table, beaming at her.

During the next year it was hard to believe that April was now Mrs. Jeff Reigle. She and Jeff had an apartment of their own, but it was only a block away and April was always popping in and out of our house almost as though she still lived there. She would arrive in the morning after Jeff left for work and sit around the kitchen chatting with Mother, or she would dash in for lunch, or she would stop by on her way to market to see if one of us wanted to go along. I was surprised at the delight she took in the apartment. At home she had never shown much liking for domestic things, but now with her own four rooms to decorate and care for she was like a child with a new toy. Mother spent a good deal of each day over at the apartment, teaching her how to do things—how to cook Jeff's favorite dishes and how to wax a wooden floor and what to do when the toilet was stopped up or the refrigerator wouldn't defrost. She and April worked together for a full week making curtains, and they would phone each other to swap recipes and talk "woman talk." It was as though, suddenly, April and Mother were on one step of a ladder and I was alone on another, and I hated it.

"You know," I said one day at dinner, "I think I'll move into April's old room. I've always liked it, and it would be nice having a window out over the garden."

Mother said, "Martha, that's ridiculous! Where on earth would you put all your books and your desk and things if you moved into April's little room?"

"I'll leave them in my old room," I said. "I can always go in and get anything I need or work at my desk in there. I'll have April's room as a bedroom and my old room as a kind of study."

"Oh, no, you don't!" exclaimed Mother. "Two rooms indeed! One of those rooms is going to be a guest room, Martha Dunning. I've never had a guest room, and I've always wanted one. You just stay in your own nice room, just as you always have."

"You'll be going away to college next year anyway," added Daddy.

"Going to college?" I repeated. I felt a wave of laughter welling up within me. For once I was going to be the center of as much astonishment, confusion and incredulous delight as April. I hesitated, wondering if this was the time to tell them. Perhaps it wasn't, but I knew I could not hold my secret any longer.

"I'm not going to college next fall," I announced triumphantly. "I'm going to be married!"

"What!"

Never in my wildest dreams had I imagined the amazement that covered their faces. I was so happy I could hardly continue.

"Yes," I said, "to Timmy. He asked me several weeks ago, but I was waiting to surprise you. His dad has promised him a job in his men's store after graduation. We're going to get an apartment, maybe in the same building with April and Jeff, and fix it all up and"—I hesitated, realizing the surprise on their faces had given way to a look that was far from the delight I had anticipated—"and everything," I finished lamely.

"Well," said Daddy as soon as I stopped talking, "you certainly are not! Throw over college and marry a shirt salesman the minute you get out of high school! That's the craziest thing I ever heard."

I felt my face growing hot with anger.

"You didn't say that when *April* wanted to get married! In fact, you did everything you possibly could to get her married to Jeff. And she wasn't a bit older than I am."

"That was different," said Mother. "Now, you just forget this getting married business, Martha Dunning, and buckle down to your studies and get yourself ready for the college entrance exams."

And that was all they would say. They refused to discuss it anymore. Timmy and I toyed with the idea of eloping, but we were both well under age and we knew our parents could have the marriage annulled as soon as they located us. Besides, when I thought about getting married I visualized a lovely wedding reception in the garden, just like April's, with Mother and Daddy beaming proudly and people surging all over the place, gasping and exclaiming about what a beautiful (well, at least "attractive") bride I was. And then the apartment with Mother making a grand fuss over me and helping me fix it up. Somehow when my parents drained all the excitement from the idea, my enthusiasm for Timmy began to wane also. By springtime we weren't even going steady any longer.

With spring came June and my graduation. I was valedictorian of our class and had a speech to make at Commencement. Mother and Daddy seemed very pleased, but at the last moment, as it turned out, even this day of glory was not fully my own. April chose that time to announce that she was going to have a baby.

"I know I should have told you sooner," she said happily, "but I thought it would be just perfect to wait and tell you tonight so the news would be a kind of special graduation present for Martha Dunning. It's due in October. Isn't it marvelous!"

"Yes," I agreed, "marvelous."

I knew in my heart that what April said was true. She had saved the news to tell tonight only because she thought I would be pleased to have it for part of my graduation excitement. Her joy was pure and complete and I knew she expected mine to be too, but it was not. Somehow the evening was no longer mine—it was April's. When I rose that night to give my speech, I looked over the audience and saw my family sitting there, watching me, but even as I spoke I saw Mother turn and look sideways at April as though wondering how she felt. And afterward, when I was preparing for bed and passed Mother's and Daddy's room on the way to the bathroom, I heard them talking. It was not about my speech or how nice I had looked in my cap and gown or how proud they were of my honors.

"A baby!" Mother was saying. "Why, she doesn't know the first thing about babies! How will she manage—the responsibility—"

"There now," Daddy said reassuringly, "it'll work out. We'll be here to help her, just as we always have. It'll be sort of nice having a baby in the family again, won't it? April's baby?"

"Yes," Mother said softly.

I went on into the bathroom and brushed my teeth so hard they bled. When I passed their door again, I did not stop to say good night; I went straight to my room and shut the door and lay there on the bed, hating April with all my might. Later there were footsteps in the hall and a light tap at my door, but I did not answer. I knew it was Mother, and I did not want to talk to her. After a few moments the footsteps went away.

That was the longest, slowest summer I can remember. Mother spent most of her time at April's apartment, cleaning and cooking and doing the things she thought it best that April not try to do. And April herself, to my disgust, had never looked lovelier.

"Martha," she said to me once, "I may never have been good in school, but I do think I'll do a good job having a baby."

'Yes," I said shortly, "you undoubtedly will."

There was no gentleness in my voice, and April looked at me in surprise. Then she smiled.

"Honestly," she said, "I think you've suffered through this pregnancy much more than I have. Martha Dunning, I've never seen you so snappish as you've been lately. Are you worried about me, honey? Please don't be. I'm just fine, really."

"No," I said truthfully, "I'm not worried about you at all."

In September college started. Mother did not go with me to buy my college wardrobe; she just had Daddy give me a check and told me to buy anything I thought I would need. Any other time the idea of such independence would have filled me with delight, but now as I drove into town I kept thinking about Mother and April, rushing about from shop to shop together, buying things for the baby. At least, I thought, Mother might have shown enough interest to want to go with me.

I shopped all day and came home with a nice assortment of clothes. Mother nodded when she saw them and said I had good taste and had found excellent values for the money, and April exclaimed over my new satin evening dress and laughed about how wonderful it would be to be able to fit into something like that again. But when they got out a bunch of little nighties they were embroidering with daisies and began to discuss whether to use pink or blue for the centers of the flowers, I went alone to carry the clothes up to my room and put them away.

The first weeks of college were pleasant ones and I

would have really enjoyed them if I had been able to relax and forget about April and all the excitement that was going on at home without me. April's baby was due the twelfth of October, and I wrote Mother that I had reservations home the afternoon of the eleventh.

"I know you'll need me," I wrote, "to help around the house and take care of April's apartment while she is in the hospital and give you both a hand with the baby when she gets it home. I can use all my semester cuts, plus the weekend, and spend a full week there."

I waited a week for what I thought would be Mother's grateful and joyful reply, but when it came it was highly unenthusiastic.

"We appreciate your wanting to help," she wrote, "but, truly, dear, the fewer people here the less confusion there will be. Besides, Jeff is going to be staying with us while April is in the hospital. Then she and the baby will stay on here until she is back on her feet again, so we will need your room. Study hard and have a good time at college, and we will telegraph you as soon as the baby arrives."

As I read the letter I felt more left out and unwanted than I ever had before, and then more angry. There was nothing to be done but sit and wait for the telegram.

The twelfth came, and the thirteenth, and the fourteenth. A week passed, and then another. And no telegram.

I burst forth with my bitterness to my roommate.

"They promised!" I raged. "They gave their word they'd telegraph me immediately!"

"Oh, don't get so upset about it," my roommate soothed. "After all, there's probably so much confusion . . . Why don't you phone them?"

I phoned that night. I meant it to be a short call. I meant to ask in a quiet, injured voice whether I had a niece or nephew. Instead, when I heard Mother's voice on the other end of the line, the anger that had been pent up in me for so long burst over and I found myself saying things I could never have imagined myself saying.

"You didn't telegraph!" I stormed. "You didn't even bother to think I might be wondering what was going on. You were so wrapped up in your precious April! All my life it's been 'April, April, April.' April gets the garden room! April gets to get married when she wants to! April gets any little thing she wants, always! Well, I'm sick and tired of it. I may not be as pretty as April but I'm your daughter too. I'm sick of April—sick to death of her—and I hope her baby turned out to be a two-headed monster!"

I clamped the receiver down on the hook and stood there in the booth, shaking with fury, and then suddenly the full horror of what I had done—of what I had said—swept over me. I leaned back against the wall of the booth and heard the words again, rasping in my ears. "I'm sick to death of April—I hope her baby—"

"No," I whispered. "Oh, no, I didn't mean that. Mother, I didn't mean that at all!"

But the receiver was back on the hook and Mother was hundreds of miles away.

I turned and went up to my dorm room, knowing that any love my parents had ever had for me would be gone after this, and I couldn't blame them. This I could not blame on April. Only on myself.

I went to class the next morning just as I always did. I can't pretend I listened carefully to the lectures. And afterward I walked over to the cafeteria and forced myself to eat a decent lunch before going back to the dorm to study. I walked to the dormitory, still alone, for my roommate had an afternoon lab, and opened the door to the room.

There, sitting in the chair by the window, was Mother.

"Mother!" I gasped. "What are you doing here! Is anything the matter! Is—"and suddenly my knees were so weak I could not stand. I stumbled forward and sat down on the end of the bed. "It's April," I whispered. "April—the baby—something happened."

Terror shot through me, sharp and icy, with a pain so great I could hardly breathe. My stomach lurched and I thought, I'm going to be sick—all that lunch I ate—and I reached out my hand crazily for the bedside table, for something to hold onto, but the table was farther away than I thought and I could not reach it. The whole room was a million miles away—the chair—the desk—even Mother, and all I could see was April's face dancing before my eyes. I could hear her laughter, bright and careless, filling the room with the sound of spring-time and see her turn to me with that puzzled expression in her eyes, the way she did when she could not understand something and wanted me to help her.

"April," I whispered. "The baby is . . ."

Mother was beside me on the bed with her arms tight around me.

"No, Martha," she was saying over and over again. "Honey, no. Nothing's the matter with April. I'm sorry I frightened you—I didn't realize—" She was shaking me, trying to get me to listen to her. "Martha, listen, dear—April's all right. The baby's overdue, that's all. It very often happens with first babies. Why, when I left last night April was at a shower over at Nancy's house."

Slowly her words penetrated and the world began to fall back into place.

"She's all right," I repeated. "And the baby—it hasn't even been born yet."

"No," said Mother. "At least, it hadn't when I left."

I stared at her. "Then what are you doing here! You left April when her baby's due any minute?"

Mother's arms were still around me. "April's all right," she said quietly. "She's got Jeff. I think my other daughter is the one who needs me right now."

I don't know exactly when I started to cry, but now I was conscious of the tears streaming down my face. I buried my face against Mother's shoulder and let them come, and it was as though all the tension and resentment and jealousy that had built up for so long were pouring out with the tears. I cried for a long time, and after I grew quiet, Mother began to talk.

"I didn't know," she said. "Until you called last night, I didn't have any idea how you felt about April. I took it for granted you understood. You're so smart, Martha Dunning—why, sometimes when you came to us with a poem you'd written or a book you wanted to discuss, Daddy and I would look at each other in amazement—we just couldn't believe that a child of ours could have a mind like yours. So maybe I assumed that you understood things when you really didn't.

"Do you remember," she asked, "the Christmas we gave you the Mickey Mouse watch?"

"No . . ." I said hesitantly, and then, "Yes." For suddenly I did remember. I had not thought of it in years, but out of the past came the memory of that wondrous moment when I pulled aside the tissue paper and saw the watch—a real one with hands that moved. "I was six years old."

"Yes." Mother nodded. "April didn't get a watch. Do you remember why?"

"She couldn't tell time," I said immediately, "and I could."

"Yes," Mother said again. "Poor April, in the second grade, and she still couldn't tell time. I think we gave her a baby doll that Christmas. But it wasn't because we loved you better that we gave you the better gift—it was because the watch was right for you and it wasn't right for April.

"No two children," she continued slowly, "are the

same. The things that are good for one may not do for another, and parents have to decide what is best for each. Sometimes they are wrong, but at least they have to try.

"When April wanted to marry Jeff it seemed like a good thing. We've always known April would marry early (can you imagine her trying to go to college or have a career?) and we were glad for it to be a mature, responsible man who would take care of her instead of one of the boys her own age. Jeff had a business right in town so we knew April would be close enough for us to help her with any problems, just as we've always done, and she could have her pretty apartment and her babies, which are all April needs to make her happy. But you, honey—why, you need more than that! You need a chance to use your mind, to see and do things by yourself, to meet boys with education and ambition! You'd go crazy with a husband who sold shirts in a men's store! You'd be bored to death with nothing to do but hem curtains and change babies. Not," she added quickly, "that you won't want babies, but you must have a chance at something else first."

She stopped and drew back a little so she could see my face.

"It had nothing to do with loving April more. Or you more. Can you see that, Martha Dunning?"

I felt so ashamed of myself I could hardly speak. "Yes," I said. "I can see."

Mother was starting to say something more when there was a quick rap at the door and one of the girls stuck her head in.

"Martha?" she said. "Is your mother in the dorm? There's a long distance call for her at the desk."

Mother practically flew into the telephone booth. It was a full five minutes later that she emerged, triumphant.

"April's baby!" she exclaimed. "It's come! A seven pound, six ounce girl! April's fine, and the delivery was an easy one. Everything's perfect!"

Her face was radiant with happiness, the same happiness she would feel, someday, at the birth of my baby. And looking at her I felt joy flowing through me—a mixture of wonder and pride and relief—and my own love for April which I had pushed from me for so long rose up within me.

"Oh", I whispered. "I'm so glad. A girl! I wonder what they will name her!"

"Well," Mother said, "that was Jeff on the phone. He says that if it's all right with you, April wants to name her baby Martha Dunning. She says she's always thought it was the most beautiful name she ever heard."

16

ROBIN HAD NEVER BEEN A HEALTHY BABY. The first three years of her life had been filled with pain and high fevers for which doctors could find no cause. Now, suddenly, she was sicker than I had ever seen her. Leaving Kerry with my parents, I flew with my older daughter to Duke Hospital in North Carolina where doctors performed immediate surgery on one of her kidneys.

Robin was in the hospital five weeks. I stayed there with her, sleeping on a cot next to her crib in the children's surgical ward. When she was finally well enough to be released, I went down to the business office to sign her out and to learn the amount of the bill.

It was staggering.

"What sort of medical insurance do you carry?" the man behind the desk asked me.

"None," I told him.

"None?" he said in surprise. "Doesn't your husband's employer offer an insurance plan?"

"My husband doesn't have an employer," I said. "He's just completed law school."

"Then, what about you? Where do you work?"

"At home," I told him. "I'm a writer."

"I didn't ask what your hobby was," the man said, "I asked where you were employed."

"I'm self-employed. I'm a professional writer."

He raised his eyes from the forms in front of him and regarded me with amusement. "How much did you earn during the past year as a result of your 'profession'?"

"Not a great deal," I admitted. "You see, I was working on books, and my agent is still in the process of marketing the manuscripts."

On the form he wrote "housewife."

"I suggest you get a job," he said. "Do you have training in anything?"

"I'm self-trained. I write."

"I'm talking about earning ability. Have you ever worked outside the home? Have you been employed *anywhere?*" He didn't wait for my answer. He could read it on my face. "You kids," he said with a sigh of exasperation. "You jump into marriage, start pumping out babies, and then expect society to give you a free ride."

"That's not true!" I objected. "We're going to pay this bill! Every time I sell a story, I'll make a payment!"

"In the meantime," the man said curtly, "I suggest you learn to wait tables."

256

I left the office after signing an agreement to pay off the horrendous hospital bill at the rate of ten dollars a month for all of eternity.

Back home in Florida, Buzz had been offered a job with a small law firm in Sarasota. Although the position had potential, the beginning pay was minimal. With the words of the man at the Duke business office ringing in my ears, I scanned the "help wanted" ads in the paper, but even the waitress jobs seemed to require experience. Besides that, I couldn't bear the thought of being away from the children. Kerry was just a toddler, and Robin was still frail and fretful from her illness and surgery. They didn't belong in a day nursery; they needed their mother.

The old nightmares returned. I was flunking, flunking, flunking. When I sat down at the typewriter, I was too depressed to be creative and stared dully for hours at a blank sheet of paper. It was true, I realized now. I was simply a "housewife." And I wasn't even a successful one. It hardly seemed worth spending time cleaning a house that my husband was never there to see or preparing meals he wasn't home to eat. If law school had been time-consuming, a law practice was apparently more so, and weekends Buzz needed for recreation. Of what that recreation consisted, I was no longer certain. I tried to tell myself it was tennis and fishing and a few drinks with his men friends, but I was beginning to suspect otherwise.

It was a weekday in midsummer when the call came. I had just finished running a load of laundry and was getting ready to lug a basket of wet clothes out to the line.

When the phone rang, I came close to not answering it. There was no one I felt like talking to, and it would probably be someone trying to sell me magazine subscriptions or asking what TV show I was watching.

But habit is strong, and ignoring a ringing phone is like turning your back on a screaming voice. I paused, then set down the clothes, and went back to pick up the receiver.

The faint, far buzz proclaimed long distance.

The voice was my agent's.

"An incredible thing has happened!" she told me. "I've just gotten word that *Debutante Hill* has been named the winner of the Seventeenth Summer Literary Award!"

"It's—what?" I said numbly.

"You've won the contest!" She sounded as stunned as I was. "There's a thousand-dollar prize, and the book will be published by Dodd, Mead and Company. *Compact Magazine* is going to serialize it, and Pyramid Books has made an offer for paperback rights."

Her voice went rattling on about the terms of the contract—an option on my next book—publicity information. I let it trickle past me. There was one fact only that was important—

I had written a book, and that book was going to be published!

"I'm an author," I whispered. "An *author!*"

I was thirteen years old again, crying, "Mother, they've bought it!"

I was "Joan" in my story "The Corner," written so many years before, standing in the sunlight, feeling myself come alive with the wonder of my own existence.

Whatever problems I might have, whatever mistakes I might have made, I was *not* worthless, *not* a failure!

I *hadn't* flunked!

"I am an *author!*" I told myself incredulously. "I am—*Lois Duncan!*"

One week later I received a second phone call. The college book had also been accepted.

If this were a work of fiction, here is where I would choose to end it. What better climax could there be than myself, clutching the phone receiver, glorying in my moment of triumph and self-discovery!

But real life does not conveniently freeze at its high points, and new chapters keep unfolding. When Robin was six and Kerry, four, I gave birth to a son, a wiry, impish little boy I named Brett Duncan. Soon after that, Buzz and I were divorced.

During the years that followed, I wrote every day,

all day, in order to support myself and the children and to pay off Duke Hospital. I taught myself kinds of writing I had never before attempted. I wrote for women's magazines, confession magazines, newspapers and religious publications; I wrote verse and advertising copy. My hobby of photography began to materialize into another source of income as I started selling photographs to magazines for illustrations and covers.

But above all, I wrote books. I did not again write short stores for teen publications. I had come to realize how much more satisfying it was to write lengthier manuscripts in which I could really develop plot and characters. The first books I wrote were romances, and then I tried a mystery-adventure story. That book was called *Ransom*, titled *Five Were Missing* when it went into paperback, and it was runner-up for the Mystery Writers of America's "Edgar Allan Poe Award." Suddenly my name began to be known to librarians.

Suddenly? That is how it may have seemed to others. In truth, there was nothing sudden about it. This was simply another "corner" of that long road I had been traveling since early childhood.

The year I wrote *Ransom*, I remarried. My husband Don is as right for me as my former husband was wrong. Don adopted my first three children, and we have two others, Don Jr. and Kate. At Don's suggestion, I returned to college. I graduated *cum laude* from the University of New Mexico, and have never had my flunking dream again. I now teach there on the faculty of the journalism department.

Several years ago one of our children began having problems in school. Although he is bright, his teachers reported that he was not paying attention in class. He did not follow instructions, and he never seemed able to remember to turn in his homework.

We had testing done, and our son was diagnosed as having a learning disability.

"There is a weakness in the area of the brain that does language processing," the educational consultant told us. "Your boy has difficulty remembering what he hears. It's not unusual for such a child to have special ability in some other area and to compensate for his deficiencies by directing all his energy into that."

"He's a talented artist," Don said. "He spends all his free time sketching."

"That figures," the consultant said. He regarded us quizzically. "Since learning disabilities are often the result of brain shape, they tend to run in families. Does either of you have a similar problem? It wouldn't necessarily have to entail *aural* memory —it might be visual or—"

"Stop right there," I told him. "You've hit the jackpot."

One year later I wrote an article on learning disabilities *Ladies' Home Journal*, the magazine that had sent me my first rejection slip, bought it for $2,500. The editor wrote me a letter praising the sensitivity of the writing and the fact that I seemed to have "such unusual understanding of what the world is like for a learning-disabled child."

My mother died before my college graduation. She did live long enough, however, to see both my brother and myself happily married. After her death, my lonely father married again. His second wife is a wonderful woman, and, for him, she too seems to have been "Written in the Stars."

For my own part, I continue to write books, most of them for teenagers.

Where do the ideas come from now that my own teen years lie behind me?

In part, from my children. The character of Mark in *Killing Mr. Griffin* is based on Robin's horrible first boyfriend. Kit, in *Down a Dark Hall*, is Kerry, and the mischievous Brendon in *A Gift of Magic* is Brett. Young Don and Kate are Neal and Megan in *Stranger with My Face*. Although none of them plans to make writing a career, four of them have published in national magazines.

Because Don's work is in New Mexico, we make our home in the Southwest, far from my beloved ocean. We go back to Florida for visits, but it isn't the same. There are high-rise condominiums where the dunes used to be, and lifeguard towers, and Popsicle sticks in the sand.

But I have not lost the world of my childhood.

draw upon it still for my books and stories, for it is a part of me and always will be.

The oldest memories are the last to go.

Song for My Mother
written after her death,
published in Good Housekeeping, *July 1971*

There is a place I used to know
Where there was sand and wind and sea—
I can remember the taste of salt
And a voice that laughed and sang to me.
I can remember a crowded room,
Warm and safe, while the wind outside
Shrieked with rage, and the angry tide
Tried time and again to reach our door;
But there was a voice, warm and low,
That laughed and said that the beach was wide.
By morning the sea was gone once more.

I haven't been there for years and years,
So long it is that I've been grown.
Now mine is the voice that laughs at fears
And sings to children of my own.
Mine is the wisdom that guards their dreams,
Yet even now when the night grows deep—
    Back I fly, back I fly,
      To sand and wind and a stretch of sky
And a quiet voice that bids me sleep.